BLACKBERRY COTTAGE

Cakes with secret ingredients
from AUBERGINE *to* ZUCCHINI

by Kate Saunders

Thank you...

If it wasn't for the following people, this book would never have materialised!
Thank you all for your support and your love – even when I got a little annoying.
Your talent and creativity are truly impressive – we are the Blackberry Cottage
dream team!!

Clare, you were the push I needed to get the whole thing started – coming up with a plan and making it work. Your design and creative flair inspired this truly wonderful design.
Strong & Together **www.sandtdesign.co.uk**

Michelle, the power of words! The most amazing copywriter who managed to put all my garbled recipe notes into a coherent order, with great quips included.
Power of Words **www.powerofwords.media**

Shannon, an incredible photographer who has an extraordinary talent for knowing just what light and colour scheme is needed to make the cakes look their absolute best.
SLR Photography **www.slr-photography.co.uk**

Chris, the most patient food stylist I know, who really, really loves icing in the heat! And who somehow managed to ice, style and skilfully cut the cakes, despite many challenges, including me! Nothing beats him.
Veni & Son **www.veniandson.co.uk**

Josie, for the loan of your beautiful crockery and props, collected over the years. Your lovely plates, bowls, cake stands and forks seemed to be endless. Thank you!

Jill, Bill and Phoebe, thank you for feeding us. I know you'll laugh when you read this – most of this book was photographed at lambing time, which meant lots of juggling whenever I had to dash off to check on a sheep! You kept us all sane when things got tough.

I would like to thank all my taste testers – your comments were invaluable, you know who you are. Thank you xx

Caroline and Edward, my mum and dad, who were always right behind me, and always there for me at the end of a phone – helping, advising or getting ingredients when I needed them.

Gemma, you are an inspiration. Your love of baking helped to create some of these cakes. You are a beautiful daughter.

Hannah, my chief recipe taster. If a cake didn't pass your taste test, it didn't go any further, back to the drawing board it went! Thank you for always being honest, even when I thought it was a good cake. You are truly a gorgeous daughter.

Lastly to Tim, my husband, without whom this would never have happened. Thank you for your endless support, love and understanding.

My dream team, thank you each and every one of you, this is for you.

Love you, Kate xxxx

PRINTED BY Printworks Global Ltd, The Barn, Milestone Cottage, Highclere, Berks RG20 9QA, England
ISBN NO. 978-1-5272-2758-3 PUBLISHED BY Blackberry Cottage

Secret ingredients within the book

Key

GF **Gluten Free**

DF **Dairy Free**

EF **Egg Free**

V **Vegan**

RSF **Refined Sugar Free**

Foreword by Bill Buckley

I first met Kate when she arrived at my radio studio to be interviewed about her baking business. I thought her idea of incorporating vegetables into sweet treats would make an interesting programme feature, but it sounded a bit gimmicky.

Fortunately, Kate had the foresight to bring one of her signature sweet potato, lemon and poppy seed cakes with her. It was absolutely delicious and I was instantly converted!

Kate has appeared on my show several times since then, always bringing bakes containing unlikely ingredients, which have invariably proved to be every bit as good as that first, ambrosial slice.

Now comes this brilliant book, in which she generously shares her best recipes – all clearly written and with mouthwatering photography – for us to bake at home.

The vegetable hater in your life won't suspect for a moment that beetroot, fennel or sweet potato is lurking in that yummy cake, tart or ice cream. And Kate's recipes are so good, you'll find yourself returning to them even when you're not only feeding vegetable lovers!

They are no more complicated to make than their traditional equivalents, are better for us and, in many cases, the surprise ingredient actually improves the texture, moistness or appearance. Talk about a win-win-win!

Cake will never be a health food, but Kate miraculously gets us halfway there, taking the guilt out of the gingerbread without ever taking the gilt off the gingerbread.

Enjoy!

Bill Buckley – Food Writer, Critic, TV & Radio Presenter

Welcome to Blackberry Cottage, home to me, my husband Tim, our two daughters Gemma and Hannah, our dog Willow, a menagerie of animals and my lovely shepherd's hut – where I bake my cakes with secret ingredients.

I've always loved vegetables. I remember as a small child eating swede my mum had just chopped – I just love the taste of raw vegetables. It was when I had children that I started adding vegetables to my cakes.

Years later, while I was working as a Sports Massage Therapist with Olympic and Paralympic teams, a client confided that she just couldn't get her child to eat vegetables, or even much fruit.

I love a challenge, and knowing how nutritionally-dense spinach is, set to work creating delicious brownies that hid a secret ingredient – a healthy vegetable.

But I didn't want just a sprinkle of spinach, I wanted the vegetable to be the biggest ingredient. I still do.

After much trial and error, I had a cake that was loved – by the child and the parents. Word spread, and soon more parents and children were asking to try my 'strange' cakes.

The next twist is thanks to my husband Tim, who convinced me to try selling my cakes at a local market. Humouring him, I baked some cakes and we set up a stall. I brought a book and settled down for a nice, uninterrupted read. But people kept stopping, trying and buying. Soon we'd sold out, my book didn't get read, and it wasn't long before I gave up Sports Massage to become a full-time baker.

Today I love what I do more than ever, and have written this book for all those people who kept asking for my recipes – OK, finally I'll share some of my secrets!

I hope this book encourages you to try something different. Please don't feel you have to follow my recipes slavishly, they're here to inspire you to try different vegetables, play with flavours and most importantly, have fun.

Happy baking
Kate x

Kate Saunders, founder of Blackberry Cottage.

Aubergine & chocolate cake

Serves 6-8

200g	aubergine
160g	unsalted butter (at room temperature)
170g	caster sugar
3	medium free-range eggs
150g	self-raising flour
3 tbsp	cocoa powder
1 tsp	baking powder
2 tsp	vanilla extract
3 tbsp	milk (any kind is fine)

Avocado & chocolate icing
See page 14

Preheat the oven to 180°C/350°F/Gas Mark 4.
Line a 20cm round loose-bottomed tin with baking parchment.

Wash and dry the aubergine, before grating coarsely. Cream the softened butter and sugar together until light and fluffy. Whisk the eggs, then add them to the butter and sugar mix a little at a time, beating the mixture as you do. Now add the grated aubergine and fold in gently.

Sift the flour, cocoa and baking powder onto the beaten egg and aubergine mixture, and gently fold in, making sure it combines well. Now you're ready to fold in the milk and vanilla extract. Try to avoid mixing too much at this stage, as you want to retain the air you sifted into the flour.

Pour into the lined tin, then bake in the middle of the preheated oven for 40 minutes, until a skewer inserted into the centre of the cake comes out clean. Carefully remove from the oven once cooked, and place on a cooling rack. When the cake's cold, gently take it out of the tin and smother in delicious avocado and chocolate icing.

Not only do aubergines add an amazing
SOFTNESS TO CAKES, *they're also*
rich in beneficial antioxidants.
Aubergines are part of the nightshade family,
which includes tomatoes and potatoes.

Aubergine, pistachio & rose cake

Serves 6-8

150g	aubergine
170g	caster sugar
3	medium free-range eggs
120ml	sunflower oil
1 tbsp	rose water
1	unwaxed lemon – juice & zest
10	cardamom pods
250g	self-raising flour
1 tsp	baking powder

Icing & decoration

150g	icing sugar
3 tsp	cold water
2 tsp	lemon juice
1 tbsp	pistachios
1 tsp	rose petals

Preheat the oven to 180°C/350°F/Gas Mark 4.
Line a 20cm round loose-bottomed tin with baking parchment.

Wash and dry the aubergine, before grating coarsely. In a large mixing bowl, whisk together the sugar, eggs and oil, then add the grated aubergine, rose water, lemon juice and zest.

Split the cardamom pods, discard the shells and crush the seeds into a fine powder in a mortar and pestle. In a separate bowl, sift the flour and baking powder, then add the crushed cardamom. Now add the flour to the aubergine and egg mixture and gently fold in, don't be too vigorous or you'll knock out the air you've sifted in.

When the mixture's ready, pour it into the lined tin and bake for 40 minutes, until a skewer inserted into the centre of the cake comes out nice and clean. Once cooked, remove from the oven and place on a cooling rack for 10 minutes, before carefully taking out of the tin to continue cooling. When the cake's cold, you're ready to decorate.

To decorate your cake

Sift the icing sugar into a bowl, add the water and lemon juice and mix until smooth. Now just pour over the cake. Don't worry about getting it perfect, I think a few runs of icing down the side looks more attractive than a completely covered cake. Crush the pistachios between your fingers, or on a board, and sprinkle over the cake, then finish with a sprinkle of rose petals.

I think this cake is extra perfect enjoyed in a garden on a summer's day with a big mug of chai tea, a delicious drink popular in Persia.

Inspired by the

PERSIAN FLAVOURS *of*

CARDAMOM, PISTACHIO AND ROSE,
I then introduced **aubergine**, *which is used
greatly in Persian cooking, to create this*

sweet, slightly spicy cake.

Avocado & chocolate icing

Makes enough to cover a 20cm round cake

1	large ripe avocado
100g	icing sugar
15g	cocoa powder

Halve the avocado and remove the stone, then scoop out the flesh and puree with a hand blender or food processor until smooth. Add the icing sugar and beat together. Once this is nicely mixed and smooth, add the cocoa powder and beat together one last time.

Now you're ready to smooth the icing over your cooled cake. Don't forget, the best helper gets to lick the spoon, and that applies if you did it all on your own.

Did you know that avocados provide
nearly 20
VITAMINS & MINERALS
in every serving.
CHOCOLATE & AVOCADO
are made for each other
- if you don't believe me, just try this recipe.

Golden beetroot, caraway seed & blackberry cake

Serves 8-10

300g	golden beetroot
170ml	sunflower oil
4	medium free-range eggs
200g	caster sugar
250g	self-raising flour
2 tsp	caraway seeds

Filling

200g	blackberries (fresh)
100g	icing sugar

Preheat the oven to 180°C/350°F/Gas Mark 4.
Line 2 x 20cm round loose-bottomed sandwich tins with baking parchment.

Begin by peeling and finely grating the raw beetroot. In a large mixing bowl, whisk together the sunflower oil, eggs and sugar until light and fluffy. Now you can add the grated beetroot and fold in gently to keep the mixture as light and fluffy as possible.

Sift the flour onto the beetroot mixture, add the caraway seeds, then gently fold in, again taking care not to knock the air out, while still making sure it's well mixed.

Pour the mixture evenly into the prepared tins. Pop into the middle of the preheated oven to bake for 20 minutes, until a skewer inserted into the centre of the cake comes out clean. Remove from the oven once cooked, and place on a cooling rack for 10 minutes before taking out of the tins.

Filling
Puree 60g of blackberries in a bowl, then push the puree through a sieve into another bowl to remove the seeds, leaving a lovely smooth puree. Add the icing sugar and mix until well combined, you might need to add more icing sugar to make it thicker.

To assemble
Cover one half of the cake with the filling, then place some of the blackberries around the outside edge, with a few in the middle to support the top layer of cake. Now you can crown with the other half of the cake, and decorate with the remaining blackberries and a dusting of icing sugar. Simply gorgeous!

GOLDEN BEETROOT

has a sweeter, milder, less earthy flavour
than its red sibling, and a wonderful
yellow colour *that will add*
A GOLDEN HUE TO YOUR CAKE.

This delicious beetroot & strawberry ice cream
IS THE PERFECT WAY TO
jazz up a sundae, **OR A SUNDAY.**

Beetroot & strawberry ice cream

GF

Makes 1 litre

200g	beetroot (fresh or vacuum packed, just not pickled!)
200g	strawberries (fresh)
2	large free-range eggs
100g	caster sugar
100ml	milk (any kind is fine)
200ml	double cream (or your preferred non-dairy alternative)

Use an ice cream maker, or make by hand in a clean 1 litre freezer-safe container.

If you're using fresh beetroot, peel and chop it before placing it into a steamer and cooking until soft, or wash halve and roast for 20 minutes to soften. If you're using vacuum-packed beetroot, it's already cooked so you can jump straight to the next step.

Place the beetroot and strawberries into a food processor or blender and blitz until you have a nice smooth puree.

In a separate bowl, whisk the eggs until light and fluffy. Add half the sugar and whisk again, before adding the rest of the sugar and whisking until all is smoothly combined. Gradually add the milk, then the cream, whisking until completely mixed in.

Now you're ready to stir in your beetroot and strawberry puree. When it's combined, place the whole lot into your ice cream maker and follow the maker's instructions.

If you're making by hand, transfer your mixture into a suitable freezer-safe container and place in the freezer for about 30 minutes, until the edges start to freeze. Take out and beat the mixture using a hand mixer or wooden spoon. By breaking up the ice cream, you're breaking up the ice crystals, which will make it smoother and creamier. Place back into the freezer and repeat after 30 minutes, and possibly once more, until it looks and feels like ice cream.

Beetroot & chocolate loaf

Serves 8-10

250g	beetroot (fresh or vacuum packed, just not pickled!)
120g	dark chocolate (70% minimum cocoa solids)
100g	unsalted butter
3	large free-range eggs
150g	caster sugar
1 tsp	vanilla extract
220g	self-raising flour
60g	cocoa powder
5 tbsp	milk (any kind is fine)

Preheat the oven to 180°C/350°F/Gas Mark 4.
Line a 900g loaf tin with baking parchment.

Pop the chocolate and butter into a heatproof bowl and place in the oven to warm through while it's preheating. While these are melting, peel (if you're using fresh beetroot) and finely grate your beetroot. When the butter and chocolate have melted, remove from the oven, stir well and set aside to cool.

Whisk the eggs and sugar together until fluffy, then gently fold in the grated beetroot and vanilla extract. Now add the cooled chocolate and butter, and fold in until well combined.

Sift the flour and cocoa powder onto the beetroot, chocolate and sugar mixture, then fold in gently, ensuring everything is well mixed. Now you're ready to gradually add the milk, folding in one tablespoon at a time to keep the mixture loose.

Pour the mixture evenly into the prepared tin, pop into the middle of the preheated oven and bake for 45 minutes, until a skewer inserted into the centre comes out clean. Carefully remove from the oven and leave on a cooling rack for 10 minutes before lifting out of the tin.

This is delicious cut into generous slices with a good dollop of crème fraiche – the slight sharpness contrasts wonderfully with the warm richness of the cake.

DID YOU KNOW...?

A hugely underrated vegetable with an exceptional nutritional value,
beetroot's sadly often only seen pickled in jars at Christmas time.
But this versatile vegetable is also

excellent boiled, roasted, raw in salads or even,
crazy thought, baked in a cake.

HERE I'VE COMBINED BEETROOT WITH CHOCOLATE
TO CREATE A LOAF CAKE THAT'S SIMPLY DELICIOUS.

Beetroot, orange & ginger loaf

Makes 1 large loaf

250g	beetroot (fresh or vacuum packed, just not pickled!)
150g	black treacle
150g	golden syrup
100g	muscovado sugar
115g	unsalted butter
2 tbsp	stem ginger syrup
100g	stem ginger
2	medium free-range eggs
2	large unwaxed oranges – juice & zest
350g	plain flour
1 tsp	bicarbonate of soda
4 tsp	ground ginger

Preheat the oven to 180°C/350°F/Gas Mark 4.
Line a 900g loaf tin with baking parchment.

While the oven's heating up, place the black treacle, golden syrup, sugar, butter and stem ginger syrup into a heatproof bowl and pop into the oven to warm through. When the butter's melted, carefully remove it from the oven, stir well, then allow to cool.

If you're using fresh beetroot, peel and halve before steaming or roasting until soft (about 20 minutes). When it's cooled, finely grate the beetroot into a bowl and add the zest and juice of the oranges. Mix together before adding the finely chopped stem ginger.

Whisk the eggs in a separate bowl, before adding to the cooled syrup mixture and combining well.

Now combine the treacle mixture with the beetroot and orange blend, and stir well.

Sift the flour, bicarbonate of soda and ground ginger onto the treacle and beetroot mixture, then fold in gently, making sure it's well mixed. Then pour evenly into the lined loaf tin.

Place the tin into the middle of the preheated oven and bake for 50 minutes, until a skewer inserted into the centre comes out clean. Remove from the oven once cooked and place on a cooling rack. Leave for 10 minutes before gently easing from the tin.

Cut thickly and enjoy just as it is.

While it's hard to resist the aroma of freshly baked Beetroot, orange & ginger loaf, this tastes even better eaten the day after being baked – it gets stickier with time.

Beetroot & raspberry jam

Makes 300g

100g	beetroot (fresh or vacuum packed, just not pickled!)
200g	raspberries (fresh or frozen)
2 tbsp	chia seeds
	maple syrup to taste

300g sterilised jam jar or Kilner jar.

If you're using fresh beetroot, either wash halve and roast for 20 minutes, or peel and chop before steaming until soft. Allow to cool before continuing.

Place the raspberries into a food processor, or use a hand blender, and blitz until smooth. Add the beetroot and blitz again, until smooth. Now add the chia seeds and, can you guess what's coming next? Blitz again! Just for a few seconds this time, until everything's nicely combined.

Have a little taste. If it's too sharp, add a little maple syrup to sweeten and blitz again for a few seconds. When you're happy with the taste, pour into your sterilised jar, and that's it. Delicious homemade beetroot and raspberry jam.

This will keep for up to a week in the fridge, although mine's always gone way before that.

Historically cultivated by the

AZTEC & MAYANS

for energy, the word chia means

'strength'. *The tiny chia seeds are*

RICH IN FIBRE, OMEGA-3, IRON,
PROTEIN AND CALCIUM.

Beetroot red velvet cake

Serves 6-8

250g	beetroot (fresh)
75ml	milk (whole or semi-skimmed)
2 tsp	lemon juice
1½ tbsp	white wine vinegar
1 tsp	vanilla extract
125g	unsalted butter (at room temperature)
2	large free-range eggs
250g	self-raising flour
150g	caster sugar
3 tbsp	cocoa powder
1½ tsp	baking powder

Cream cheese frosting

200g	cream cheese
300g	icing sugar
2 tsp	vanilla extract

Preheat the oven to 180°C/350°F/Gas Mark 4.
Line 2 x 15cm round loose-bottomed sandwich tins with baking parchment.

This stunning cake is deceptively easy to make and super delicious to eat. Begin by placing the milk and 2 teaspoons of the lemon juice into a small jug, then set aside. Next comes the finger-colouring peeling and fine chopping of the raw beetroot. Place into a bowl and add the milk and lemon, plus the white wine vinegar and vanilla. Pop the whole lot into a food processor, or use a hand blender, and blitz until you have a fine, silky-smooth puree.

Add the butter to the puree and give it another good blitz. Then add the eggs and, you've got it, blitz again until everything's nicely combined and smooth.

Lastly, sift the flour, sugar, cocoa powder and baking powder onto your puree and mix well until everything is combined. Now divide the mixture evenly between the two lined tins and pop into the oven to bake for 30-40 minutes, until a skewer inserted into the centre of a cake comes out clean. Once cooked, place on a cooling rack for 10 minutes before gently removing the tins and allowing the cakes to cool completely.

Now for the light fluffy cream cheese frosting
Place the cream cheese into a bowl with a small amount of icing sugar and blend together, gradually adding more icing sugar until it's all combined. Now add the vanilla extract and mix well together.

Assembling your masterpiece
Begin by slicing the two cakes across the middle to create four rounds. Spread some of your frosting evenly across the top of three rounds. Stack the frosted rounds, placing the un-iced round on top, and spread the rest of the frosting over the whole cake. Now step back and admire your masterpiece.

A little red velvet cake history

The cake and its original recipe are well known in the United States. The name is believed to come from the sugar of the time, combined with the unprocessed cocoa powder, that created a lovely red hue.

Traditionally, the cake was iced with a very light and fluffy French-style butter roux icing (also called ermine icing). Over time, this has been replaced by increasingly popular cream cheese and buttercream frosting variations.

During World War II, food rationing led bakers to use boiled beetroot flesh and juice to add moisture and enhance the colour of their cakes, creating wonderfully vibrant red cakes.

Butternut squash & apricot torte

Serves 8-10

250g	butternut squash
50g	unsalted butter (at room temperature)
50g	caster sugar
3	medium free-range eggs
3 tbsp	clear runny honey
1 tsp	vanilla extract
100g	dried apricots
150g	plain flour
1 tsp	baking powder
50g	ground almonds
2 tbsp	flaked almonds

Preheat the oven to 180°C/350°F/Gas Mark 4.
Line a 20cm round loose-bottomed tin with baking parchment.

Peel and finely grate the butternut squash. Save the peel and seeds to roast for a tasty snack (see page 144).

In a large mixing bowl, cream together the butter and sugar. Add the eggs one at a time and keep beating to ensure a smooth mixture. Now stir in the honey and vanilla extract, mixing well until all are combined. Dice the apricots and mix with the grated butternut squash, before adding to the butter and honey mixture, stirring well to ensure everything is evenly combined.

Sift the flour, baking powder and ground almonds onto the butternut squash mixture, then fold in gently, ensuring everything is thoroughly combined. Pour evenly into the prepared tin. Sprinkle with the flaked almonds and place in the middle of the preheated oven to bake for 30-40 minutes, until a skewer inserted into the centre comes out clean. Carefully remove from the oven once cooked and place on a cooling rack for 10 minutes, before removing from the tin.

I like to serve this with a slice of fresh apricot and a generous dollop of crème fraiche, the contrasting flavours are delicious together.

DRIED APRICOTS *looking a bit dark and dull?*
Good, *that means they've been* AIR DRIED.
The bright orange dried apricots have been treated with sulphur dioxide.

Butternut squash & honey cake

Serves 6-8

200g	butternut squash
250g	clear runny honey
200g	unsalted butter
100g	dark brown sugar
300g	self-raising flour
2	large free-range eggs

Glaze

2 tbsp	clear runny honey

Preheat the oven to 160°C/325°F/Gas Mark 3.
Line a 20cm round loose-bottomed tin with baking parchment.

Peel and finely grate the butternut squash. See page 144 for tasty seed and skin snack ideas.
Place the honey, butter and sugar into a pan and melt gently over a low heat, making sure that
the sugar has dissolved. Mix in the grated butternut squash and set aside to cool.

Now sift the flour into a separate bowl, make a well in the middle and add the cooled
butternut squash and honey mixture. Combine well. Add the eggs and mix again, until
everything is nicely combined.

Pour the mixture evenly into the prepared tin and place it in the middle of the preheated
oven to bake for 50 minutes, until a skewer inserted into the centre comes out clean and the
cake springs back when pressed. Remove from the oven once cooked and place on a cooling
rack for 10 minutes, before taking out of the tin.

Glazed and good to go

While you're waiting for the cake to cool, heat the 2 tablespoons of honey in a small saucepan
over a low heat until it's warmed through (or in a microwaveable bowl, on low, for 40 seconds).
Brush the honey over the cake, using a pastry brush, for a tasty glaze. Now just leave to cool.

If you can resist the temptation, this tastes
even better eaten the next day
IT GETS STICKER WITH TIME.
Try a slice warmed in the microwave,
with a drizzle of honey,
it's delicious.

ANTIOXIDANT BUTTERNUT SQUASH
has great skin and eyesight health benefits.
Nothing's wasted either, the skin and seeds can
be eaten as a nutritious snack.

Butternut squash, orange & almond cake

Serves 8-10

200g	butternut squash
1	large unwaxed orange
150g	unsalted butter (at room temperature)
160g	light brown sugar
3	medium free-range eggs
170g	self-raising flour
½ tsp	bicarbonate of soda
50g	ground almonds

To decorate

1	handful of toasted flaked almonds
1	slice of crystallised orange
15g	icing sugar (enough for a dusting)

Preheat the oven to 180°C/350°F/Gas Mark 4.
Line a 20cm round loose-bottomed tin with baking parchment.

Get the butter out of the fridge to soften. Peel and finely grate the butternut squash. You can roast the seeds, they make a lovely tasty snack (see page 144 for more on this).

Cut the orange into small pieces. Don't worry about peeling, it all goes in, just remove any pips, then blitz in a food processor, or with a hand blender, until it forms a smooth puree. Mix the orange puree and grated butternut squash together.

Place the softened butter, sugar and eggs into a bowl and cream together. Now add the orange and butternut squash fusion and thoroughly combine.

In a separate bowl, sift together the flour, bicarbonate of soda and ground almonds. Fold this into the creamed butter and sugar mixture, making sure everything is well mixed. Now just pour evenly into the prepared tin and pop into the middle of the preheated oven. Bake for 25 minutes, until the cake is well risen and a skewer inserted into the centre comes out clean. Once cooked, remove from the oven and place on a cooling rack for 5 minutes before taking out of the tin. Leave to continue cooling before decorating.

To decorate

This couldn't be simpler to decorate, and the finished cake looks fantastic. All you do is scatter some flaked almonds on top and dust with icing sugar, place the crystallised orange in the middle of the cake, and that's it. Enjoy.

Savoy cabbage mocha torte

Serves 8-10

150g	savoy cabbage
150g	dark chocolate (70% minimum cocoa solids)
150g	unsalted butter
1 tbsp	instant coffee
1 tbsp	boiling water
3	large free-range eggs
150g	caster sugar
70g	self-raising flour
70g	ground almonds

Preheat the oven to 180°C/350°F/Gas Mark 4.
Line a 20cm round loose-bottomed tin with baking parchment.

Begin by washing and roughly chopping the cabbage. Steam until soft, then puree until smooth with a hand blender or food processor. You might need to add a tablespoon of water to help it puree, just don't add too much.

While the oven's preheating, break the chocolate into a heatproof bowl, add the butter and pop into the oven. When it's melted, carefully remove and stir well.

In a small cup, stir 1 tablespoon of boiling water into the coffee, then add this to the butter and chocolate mixture and stir well before leaving to cool.

Now you're ready to whisk the eggs and sugar together, until light and fluffy in consistency. Fold in the cooled pureed cabbage, taking care not to knock out any of the air you just whisked in. Next gently fold in the cooled chocolate mixture. Keep folding, this time adding the sifted flour and ground almonds, the last of the ingredients.

Finally, you're ready to pour the mixture evenly into the prepared tin, before placing it into the middle of a preheated oven to bake for 40 minutes. You can tell it's ready when a skewer inserted into the centre comes out a little sticky with mixture. Remove from the oven and place on a rack to cool completely before removing the tin.

If you have any chocolate coffee beans, add a few to the top, these are the perfect addition and add a lovely crunch.

Savoy cabbage has quite a different texture and appearance to white, spring or green cabbage. The flavour's different too, it's more delicate. NUTRIENT-RICH SAVOY CABBAGE **is also a fantastic source of fibre and vitamins B, C & K,** *among many others.* IT REALLY IS ALL GOOD!

Spring greens & apple loaves

Cabbage has a clear affinity with apple, which in this case, makes for cake perfection.

Makes 10 mini loaves

200g	spring greens
50ml	apple juice
2	medium apples
100ml	sunflower oil
2	large free-range eggs
150g	caster sugar
250g	self-raising flour
1 tsp	baking powder
1 tsp	ground cinnamon

Preheat the oven to 180°C/350°F/Gas Mark 4.
Use prepared mini loaf cases, so you just need to fill them.

Wash and finely slice the spring greens, discarding any hard stalks, then steam until soft. When ready, move to a bowl, add the apple juice, then puree with a hand blender or food processor until smooth.

While the cabbage puree is cooling, you can coarsely grate the apples, taking care to mind your fingertips! Whisk together the sunflower oil, eggs and sugar until light and fluffy. Add the cooled spring greens puree and grated apples to the mixture, then fold in gently.

Sift the flour, baking powder and ground cinnamon onto your mixture, then gently fold in until nicely combined. Pour evenly into your mini loaf cases and bake on the middle shelf for 15-20 minutes, until a skewer inserted into the centre of a loaf comes out clean. Remove from the oven and place onto a cooling rack.

These little loaves are perfect for picnics and lunch boxes. You can make them in batches and freeze them so you've a ready supply.

Sweetheart cabbage cinnamon rolls

EF

Makes 14 rolls

Filling

100g	sweetheart cabbage
60g	unsalted butter (at room temperature)
60g	light brown sugar
2 tsp	cinnamon
60g	sultanas
60g	currants

Roll

340g	self-raising flour
40g	unsalted butter (diced)
1 tsp	ground cinnamon
200ml	milk (any kind is fine)

Glaze

6 tbsp	water
20g	caster sugar

Preheat the oven to 180°C/350°F/Gas Mark 4.
Line a 23cm tin with baking parchment, then grease and flour the sides.

We're going to make the filling first. Finely chop the sweetheart cabbage and steam until soft. Place the softened butter, sugar and cinnamon in a bowl and cream together. Place to one side.

Now we'll make the roll dough. Place the flour, diced butter and cinnamon into a bowl and rub lightly together with your fingertips, until it forms the consistency of breadcrumbs. Next add the milk and keep mixing until you have a firm dough. Remove from the bowl, place on a lightly floured surface and knead until you have a smooth dough.

Getting ready to roll

Roll the dough into an oblong shape, about ½cm thick. Spread the creamed butter and sugar over the dough. Sprinkle with sultanas and currants, followed by the cooled steamed cabbage. Now you're ready to roll.

Starting at the longest side, carefully roll the dough and filling into a long sausage. Then, using a sharp knife, cut your roll into 14 even slices or rounds.

Place the rounds side by side in the prepared tin, they should be starting to look like cinnamon rolls now. Bake in the middle of the preheated oven for 20 minutes, until golden brown.

While the rolls are baking, it's the perfect time to prepare the glaze. Place the water and sugar into a saucepan and simmer until the sugar has melted. When the rolls are ready, remove them from the oven and brush with the glaze while they're still hot. Allow to cool as much as possible before diving in.

I like these with a big mug of coffee, which is very popular in Slovakia, but they go equally well with just about anything.

My cinnamon rolls **with a twist** are inspired by a

TRADITIONAL SLOVAK RECIPE.

Cabbage is a popular ingredient in **Eastern Europe**,
being prepared and eaten in a variety of different ways.

It also adds a unique tasty twist to your cinnamon rolls.

For a carrot cake with a difference, why not try
PURPLE OR YELLOW CARROTS,
they taste **EQUALLY LOVELY.**

Classic carrot cake

The classic carrot cake that we all know and love.

Serves 8-10

100g	carrots
80g	sultanas
1	unwaxed orange – juice & zest
90ml	sunflower oil
90g	light brown sugar
2	medium free-range eggs
30g	walnuts
75g	self-raising flour
75g	wholemeal flour
½ tsp	bicarbonate of soda
½ tsp	ground cinnamon
½ tsp	mixed spice

Cream cheese frosting

100g	icing sugar
100g	cream cheese
1 tsp	vanilla extract

Preheat the oven to 180°C/350°F/Gas Mark 4.
Line a 900g loaf tin with baking parchment.

Soak the sultanas in the orange juice and zest, while you make the rest of the cake mix.

Wash and finely grate the carrots, minding your fingers! Place the oil and sugar into a bowl and mix together, then add the eggs and mix again.

Now you're ready to add the grated carrots, walnuts, soaked sultanas and orange juice to the sugar mixture, stirring until all are nicely combined. Sift the two types of flour, bicarbonate of soda, cinnamon and mixed spice directly onto the mixture. Stir thoroughly, then pour evenly into the prepared tin.

Place the tin in the middle of the preheated oven and bake for 40 minutes, until a skewer inserted into the centre comes out clean. Remove from the oven and place on a cooling rack for 10 minutes, before removing the tin.

Topping the carrot cake

A cream cheese frosting is the perfect topping for a classic carrot cake. Place the icing sugar, cream cheese and vanilla extract into a bowl and cream together. I like to use a wooden spoon for this. Once the cake is cool, spread your frosting over the top of the cake. And that's it, a super tasty frosted carrot cake.

Carrot & cardamom ice cream

Makes 1 litre

300g	carrots
100ml	milk (any kind is fine)
100g	runny honey
2	cardamom pods
2	large free-range eggs
200ml	double cream (or your preferred non-dairy alternative)

Use an ice cream maker, or make by hand in a clean 1 litre freezer-safe container.

Peel the carrots and chop into small cubes, place in a saucepan with half the milk, half the honey and both cardamom pods. Bring to the boil and simmer until the carrots are soft and most of the liquid has been absorbed, then set aside to cool.

Once cooled, lift out the cardamom pods and carefully squash them until they open and the seeds can be removed. Discard the shells.

Pop the carrots, cardamom seeds and any milk left in the saucepan into a food processor or blender, and blitz until you have a smooth paste.

In a separate bowl, whisk the eggs and remaining honey together until light and fluffy. Gradually add the cream and remaining milk, and whisk slowly until completely combined. Stir in your carrot puree, mixing well to ensure the ingredients are evenly combined, then pour the mix into your ice cream maker and follow the maker's instructions.

If you're making by hand, transfer your mixture into a suitable freezer-safe container and place in the freezer for about 30 minutes, until the edges start to freeze. Take out and beat the mixture using a hand mixer or wooden spoon. By breaking up the ice cream, you're breaking up the ice crystals, which will make it smoother and creamier. Place back into the freezer and repeat after another 30 minutes, and possibly once more, until it looks and feels like ice cream.

I serve this quite often, it makes a lovely end to a dinner and always gets devoured.

THIS FRUITY FEAST
goes brilliantly with just about everything
BUT MY FAVOURITE IS A BIG MUG OF
BREAKFAST TEA & A MOMENT OF CALM.

Carrot cake ice cream

Combining carrots with juicy sultanas and delicious spices creates this wonderful carrot cake ice cream.

Makes 1 litre

300g	carrots
2	large free-range eggs
100g	caster sugar
1 tsp	ground cinnamon
1 tsp	ground or freshly grated nutmeg
100ml	milk (any kind is fine)
200ml	double cream (or your preferred non-dairy alternative)
20g	sultanas

Use an ice cream maker, or make by hand in a clean 1 litre freezer-safe container.

Wash, peel and roughly chop the carrots, and steam until soft. Transfer to a food processor or blender, and blitz until you have a smooth puree.

In a separate bowl, whisk the eggs together until light and fluffy. Add half the sugar and whisk again, then add the rest of the sugar and whisk until all is combined. Add your spices, then gradually add the milk and cream, whisking slowly as you do to ensure everything is thoroughly mixed together.

Finally, stir in your carrot puree and sultanas, and once these are nicely combined, pour the mix into your ice cream maker and follow the manufacturer's instructions.

If you're making by hand, transfer your mixture into a suitable freezer-safe container and place in the freezer for about 30 minutes, until the edges start to freeze. Take out and beat the mixture using a hand mixer or wooden spoon. By breaking up the ice cream, you're breaking up the ice crystals, which will make it smoother and creamier. Place back into the freezer and repeat after another 30 minutes, and possibly once more, until it looks and feels like ice cream.

This looks stunning served in a sundae glass with chunks of carrot cake, as a carroty knickerbocker glory.

Carrot mincemeat

Makes 500g

60g	carrot
100g	apple
100g	sultanas
100g	raisins
50g	cranberries
100g	currants
50g	dark brown sugar
80g	vegetable suet
1 tsp	mixed spice
1	unwaxed orange – juice & zest
50ml	Cointreau

2 x 300g sterilised jam jars or Kilner jars.

Wash and peel both the carrot and apple, then finely grate the carrot and coarsely grate the apple.

In a separate bowl, mix all of the dried ingredients. Now add the sugar, suet and spice, and mix well. Finally, add the orange juice and zest, Cointreau, grated carrot and apple. Give everything a good stir to ensure it's all well mixed.

Cover with a tea towel and leave in a cool, dry place for at least 24 hours, remembering to give the mix a good stir whenever you're passing. Spoon into clean sterilised jars, packing the mix down with the back of a teaspoon.

This will keep for up to 6 months in a cool, dry place, such as a pantry, larder, or even under the stairs.

Mincemeat

CARROTS HAVEN'T ALWAYS BEEN ORANGE.
In fact, it was the Dutch
who created the orange carrot in the 17th century,
as a tribute to William of Orange.
Before then, carrots were yellow, white,
red & even purple.

Carrot, sultana & apple cake

Serves 6-8

140g	carrots
80g	sultanas
1	unwaxed orange – juice & zest
1	medium apple
30ml	sunflower oil
100g	light brown sugar
200g	wholemeal self-raising flour
½ tsp	baking powder
1 tsp	ground cinnamon

Preheat the oven to 180°C/350°F/Gas Mark 4.
Line a 20cm round loose-bottomed tin with baking parchment.

Begin by soaking the sultanas in the orange juice and zest. While they're soaking, you can get on with the rest of the recipe.

Wash and finely grate the carrot, then wash and coarsely grate the apple. Place the oil and sugar into a bowl and mix together. Now add the grated carrot and apple, soaked sultanas and orange, and mix well.

Sift the flour, baking powder and cinnamon onto the carrot and apple mixture, then stir well until all the ingredients are thoroughly combined.

Pour the mixture evenly into the prepared tin, pop into the middle of the preheated oven and bake for 50 minutes, until a skewer inserted into the centre comes out clean. Set aside on a cooling rack and carefully remove from the tin after 10 minutes. No need to decorate, I think this is perfect simply as it is.

Carrot Christmas pudding

The secret to this Christmas treat with a twist, is to make it at least 6 weeks before Christmas, to allow the pudding to mature nicely. I pop a note on the calendar in October to remind me.

**Makes a 900g pudding
– enough for 8-10 people**

200g	carrots	1 tsp	ground cinnamon
120g	sultanas	1 tsp	ground coriander
120g	raisins	1 tsp	ground or freshly grated nutmeg
100g	currants	2	unwaxed oranges – juice & zest
40g	mixed peel	100ml	brandy or sherry
50g	mixed nuts	1	large apple
½ tsp	cloves	30g	breadcrumbs
		50g	vegetable suet
		80g	plain flour

One traditional Christmas pudding bowl, with a good lip for securing the string around the outside, and grooves on the base to release trapped air during steaming. You'll also need string, greaseproof paper and foil.

Place the sultanas, raisins, currants, mixed peel, nuts and spices into a large bowl, stir well, add the orange juice, zest and brandy or sherry, then leave overnight for the fruit to plump.

The next day, wash and finely grate the carrot, wash and coarsely grate the apple, then mix them both into the soaked fruits, until all the ingredients are thoroughly combined. Now mix in the breadcrumbs and suet, sift on the flour and give the whole lot a thorough mix.

Pour the mixture into the pudding bowl, press down firmly, then cover with a pleated sheet of greaseproof paper. Secure tightly around the outside of the bowl with string.

Steam the covered pudding bowl for about 4½ hours, regularly checking and topping up the water as needed. If you don't have a steamer, put the pudding into a colander and cover securely with foil, so that no steam escapes, then steam over a saucepan. Cool completely on a rack. Cover with a fresh sheet of greaseproof paper, tie with string, then wrap the whole bowl in foil. Leave to mature in a cool, dry place, ideally for 6 weeks.

To reheat
Steaming for 2 hours is best, as the pudding comes out lovely and moist. If you prefer to microwave, put a small cup of water beside the pudding for added moisture, heat on full power for 2 minutes, rest for 1 minute, then full again for 1 minute. Check the middle's piping hot.

To serve
Unwrap with care, it'll be very hot. Turn out onto a serving dish, douse with brandy or sherry and either set alight or simply enjoy with your favourite sauce, butter, cream or custard.

A lucky find

Adding a silver coin to the pudding mix is an age-old custom, said to bring prosperity to the lucky person who finds it. In the UK, a silver sixpence was traditionally used.

A treat fit for an Olympian

There is evidence that cheesecake was served to athletes during the first ancient Olympic games in 776 BC, as it was a good source of energy. They used to bake it under hot stones.

Cauliflower & blackberry cheesecake

Cauliflower also comes in green, orange and purple varieties. It's definitely worth playing around with other coloured vegetables in this and other recipes.

Serves 8-10

Base

70g	unsalted butter
1	unwaxed orange – juice & zest
1 tsp	caster sugar
200g	spelt flour
50g	whole rolled oats
½ tsp	ground or freshly grated nutmeg

Filling

150g	cauliflower florets
200g	blackberries
2 tbsp	water
500g	cream cheese
150g	caster sugar
2	medium free-range eggs
50g	plain flour

Preheat the oven to 180°C/350°F/Gas Mark 4.
Line the base of a 20cm springform cake tin with baking parchment and grease the sides.

Starting with the base, melt the butter, orange juice, zest and sugar together in a saucepan over a low heat. Place the flour, oats and nutmeg into a bowl, then stir in the melted butter mixture until it looks like breadcrumbs. Now pour the mixture into your tin and press down firmly with the back of a spoon. Bake for 10 minutes, until it's a light golden colour, then set to one side.

Filling

While your base is cooling, you can make the filling. Place the blackberries and water into a small saucepan, heat until soft and pulpy, then puree until smooth. Finish by pushing the puree through a sieve to remove the pips, and allow to cool.

Finely chop the cauliflower, or blitz with a food processor or hand blender until it looks like breadcrumbs. In a separate bowl, beat the cream cheese and sugar until smooth. Slowly add the eggs, beating after each addition, then fold in the cauliflower crumbs. Now sift on the flour and fold in, then gently fold in half the blackberry puree.

Pour the mixture evenly over the base. Pop into the middle of the preheated oven and bake for 30 minutes. To check if it's cooked, tap the side of the tin with a metal spoon, the centre should be slightly soft and wobbly – you don't want it to overbake or you'll lose the lovely creaminess of the cheesecake. Transfer to a rack, the centre will keep cooking even as the outside starts to cool. When completely cool, lift from the tin and refrigerate until needed.

The finishing flourish

When you're ready to serve, pour the last of the blackberry puree over the top and spread out with a palette knife. I love to serve this with blackberries and a spoonful of mascarpone.

Cauliflower, espresso & walnut Swiss roll

Cauliflower

Serves 6-8

Roll

100g	cauliflower
4 tbsp	strong coffee (espresso works well)
30g	walnuts
70g	caster sugar
3	medium free-range eggs
70g	self-raising flour

Filling

80g	unsalted butter (at room temperature)
175g	icing sugar
1 tbsp	strong coffee (espresso works well)

Preheat the oven to 200°C/400°F/Gas Mark 6.
Line a 33cm x 23cm Swiss roll tin with baking parchment.

We'll start with the roll. Chop the cauliflower into small bits and blitz with the coffee in a food processor, or with a hand blender, until smooth.

Very finely chop the walnuts. Set to one side while you whisk the sugar and eggs together until light and fluffy. Now you're ready to fold in the cauliflower, coffee and walnuts.

Sift the flour onto the whisked cauliflower, coffee and egg mixture, then gently fold in. When nicely combined, pour the whole lot evenly into your prepared Swiss roll tin. Pop into the middle of the preheated oven and bake for 8-10 minutes, until it's golden brown and a skewer inserted into the centre of the cake comes out clean.

When it's ready, carefully turn the cake out onto a lightly sugared piece of greaseproof paper. Peel off the baking parchment and neaten the edges with a quick trim, if required. Allow to cool for 3 minutes – don't let it get cold or it'll be difficult to roll.

Score one short side with a sharp knife, about 1cm from the edge. Then, using the greaseproof paper, roll up from the scored side, and leave seam-side down to finish cooling.

Now for the filling

Cream the butter and icing sugar together in a bowl until light and fluffy, then gradually add the tablespoon of coffee, still beating to ensure a nice even mix.

The final stage, building your Swiss roll

Unroll the sponge then, using a palette knife, spread the filling evenly over the inner surface. Using the greaseproof paper, carefully roll the sponge back up, placing it seam-side down. Transfer to a plate, sprinkle with icing sugar and top with coffee beans, then take a moment to admire your creation. Enjoy!

A cruciferous vegetable, CAULIFLOWER HAS SIGNIFICANT LEVELS OF NUTRIENTS. Its white flesh is also known as 'curd' due to its cheese curd appearance.

ORANGES & LEMONS

SAY THE BELLS OF ST CLEMENTS,
only now with an added twist,
nutritious cauliflower.

Cauliflower St Clements cake

Serves 8-10

200g	cauliflower florets
1	unwaxed lemon – juice & zest
1	unwaxed orange – juice & zest
2 tsp	vanilla extract
1	medium free-range egg
125ml	sunflower oil
120g	caster sugar
200g	self-raising flour
1 tsp	baking powder

Filling & icing

4 tbsp	mascarpone
2 tbsp	lemon curd
1 tbsp	icing sugar

Preheat the oven to 180°C/350°F/Gas Mark 4.
Line 3 x 20cm round loose-bottomed tins with baking parchment.

Finely chop the cauliflower, or blitz in a food processor until it looks like breadcrumbs. Pour into a bowl and set aside.

Zest and then juice both the lemon and orange, then add to the cauliflower crumbs, with the vanilla extract, and stir well.

In a separate bowl, whisk the eggs, sunflower oil and sugar together until light and fluffy. Add the cauliflower mixture and gently fold in. Now sift the flour and baking powder on top, and fold in gently until everything is evenly combined.

Pour the mixture evenly into the prepared tins, pop into the middle of the preheated oven and bake for 20-30 minutes, until a skewer inserted into the centre comes out clean. Now just place on a cooling rack, wait 10 minutes, then gently remove from the tins. Allow the cakes to finish cooling completely before assembling and decorating.

Bringing it all together
Mix the mascarpone, lemon curd and icing sugar together. Spread half the filling over the tops of two of the cakes, taking it all the way to the edges, then stack all three cakes before smoothing the remaining filling over your assembled cake. Decorate with a sprinkle of zest, edible flowers such as pretty violas, and even a fun couple of cauliflower florets.

Celeriac & cherry Madeira cake

Serves 6-8

150g	celeriac
160g	unsalted butter (at room temperature)
160g	caster sugar
3	medium free-range eggs
100g	glacé cherries
200g	self-raising flour
4 tbsp	milk (any kind is fine)

Preheat the oven to 170°C/325°F/Gas Mark 3.
Line a 20cm round loose-bottomed tin with baking parchment.

Peel and finely grate the celeriac. In a large mixing bowl, cream together the softened butter and sugar until light and fluffy.

Crack the eggs into a separate bowl and break up with a fork. Gradually add the eggs to the butter and sugar mixture, beating continually as you do. Now add the celeriac and mix gently with a wooden spoon or a spatula, until all the ingredients are nicely combined.

Toss the cherries in a little of the flour until they're covered. Set to one side for now.

Going back to the celeriac mixture, sift the rest of the flour onto the mix and fold in gently, until the ingredients are thoroughly combined. Now gently fold in the cherries, then gradually add the milk, again folding in gently.

Pour the mixture into the lined tin and bake on the middle shelf of the preheated oven for 50 minutes. After 30 minutes, check on the cake – if it's browning too quickly, cover it with a piece of baking parchment for the remaining time. You can tell it's done when a skewer inserted into the centre of the cake comes out clean. If there's still mixture on the skewer, leave for another 5 minutes and check again. Repeat until the skewer comes out clean.

Remove from the oven once cooked and place on a cooling rack for 15 minutes before removing from the tin. Serve just as is, or with a light dusting of icing sugar and a couple of cherries.

This can also be made in a 900g loaf tin, and is a sure winner in a picnic hamper.

Beauty in the beast

I love ugly veg, and CELERIAC, WITH ITS ODD KNOBBLY SHAPE, IS MY UNSUNG HERO. *The lumpy exterior hides a lovely celery-like flavour with a subtle nuttiness, and as for its fantastic health benefits, it's packed full of goodness.*

Celeriac & pear cake

Serves 6-8

200g	celeriac
2	pears
½ tbsp	caster sugar
150g	coconut oil
120g	caster sugar
3	medium free-range eggs
1 tsp	vanilla extract
150g	ground almonds
120g	rice flour
½ tsp	baking powder

Preheat the oven to 180°C/350°F/Gas Mark 4.
Grease the sides of a 20cm springform cake tin and line the base with
baking parchment.

Peel and finely grate the celeriac. Peel, core and thickly slice the pears. Sprinkle the half tablespoon of caster sugar over the base of your tin and arrange the pear slices so they cover the base – these will become the top of your cake, so have fun arranging them.

Beat the coconut oil and sugar together until they're light and fluffy. In a separate bowl, break the eggs up with a fork, then add them gradually to your coconut oil and sugar blend, gently beating after each addition. Now mix in the vanilla extract, then gently fold in the grated celeriac.

Sift the ground almonds, rice flour and baking powder onto your mixture, then gently fold in. Now pour this evenly over the pears, before placing in the middle of the preheated oven to bake for 30 minutes, or until a skewer inserted into the centre of the cake comes out clean.

Remove from the oven once cooked and place onto a cooling rack. After 10 minutes, turn the tin upside down and remove, and ta da, the pears are now on top and you have a delicious self-decorated cake.

Celeriac, rum & raisin cake

Serves 6-8

200g   celeriac
4 tbsp   rum
100g   raisins
1   apple
200g   self-raising flour
½ tsp   baking powder
1 tsp   mixed spice
140g   light brown sugar
150ml   sunflower oil

Preheat the oven to 180°C/350°F/Gas Mark 4.
Line a 20cm round loose-bottomed tin with baking parchment.

Place the raisins in a bowl, cover with the rum and leave to steep while you make the rest of the cake.

Peel and finely grate the celeriac, then coarsely grate the apple and add to the celeriac. In a separate bowl, mix the sugar and sunflower oil together until nicely combined.

Add the rum and rum-plumped raisins to the grated celeriac and apple, and mix well before adding the sugar and oil mixture, stirring continuously until all the ingredients are thoroughly combined. Now sift the flour, baking powder and mixed spice on top, and stir well to ensure a nice even cake mixture.

Pour the mixture evenly into the prepared tin, sprinkle with a few raisins, then pop into the middle of the preheated oven to bake for 45 minutes, or until a skewer inserted into the centre of the cake comes out clean. When it's ready, place on a cooling rack and leave for 10 minutes before removing the tin, then leave to cool completely.

This is a wonderful vegan cake – a real tea time treat packed with fruit and vegetables.

Cucumber & Pimm's cake

Serves 6-8

100g	cucumber
2 tbsp	Pimm's
100g	unsalted butter (at room temperature)
125g	caster sugar
2	medium free-range eggs
150g	self-raising flour
½ tsp	baking powder

Pimm's syrup

2 tbsp	Pimm's
100g	caster sugar

Decoration

Fresh strawberries, cucumber slices and a few mint leaves

Preheat the oven to 170°C/325°F/Gas Mark 3.
Line a 20cm round loose-bottomed tin with baking parchment.

Wash and finely grate the cucumber, then leave in a sieve to drain. Cream the Pimm's, butter and sugar until light and fluffy. Crack the eggs into a cup and break up with a fork, before gradually beating into the Pimm's, butter and sugar mix. When that's combined, gently fold in the grated cucumber.

Sift the flour and baking powder into a separate bowl, then fold into the Pimm's and cucumber mixture, until everything is nicely combined.

Pour the mixture evenly into your prepared tin and place in the middle of the preheated oven to bake for 35 minutes, or until a skewer inserted into the centre of the cake comes out clean.

While the cake's baking, you can prepare the Pimm's syrup. Pour the Pimm's and sugar into a saucepan and heat gently until the sugar has dissolved. That's it, your work is almost done, and this seems like an ideal time to mix an accompanying glass of Pimm's.

When the cake's baked, place it on a cooling rack. While it's still in the tin, use a skewer to prick the surface of the cake, then spoon over the syrup. Allow the cake to finish cooling completely, and the syrup to soak in, before taking it out of the tin and decorating with strawberries, sliced cucumber and mint leaves.

This cake is what summers were made for.

Cucumber & rose loaves

Makes 6 mini loaves

100g	cucumber
2	large free-range eggs
100g	caster sugar
120ml	sunflower oil
1 tsp	vanilla extract
2 tsp	rose water
200g	self-raising flour
½ tsp	bicarbonate of soda
½ tsp	baking powder

Drizzle icing

50g	icing sugar
1 tsp	beetroot juice (from a vacuum pack or beetroot juice drink)
1 tsp	rose water
	sprinkling of rose petals (unsprayed – ideally from your own garden if possible)

Preheat the oven to 180°C/350°F/Gas Mark 4.
Use prepared mini loaf cases, so you just need to fill them.

Wash and finely grate the cucumber, then leave it in a sieve to drain – cucumber is naturally high in water, and you don't want loaves with soggy bottoms.

In a large mixing bowl, whisk together the eggs, sugar and oil until light and fluffy. Now add the cucumber, vanilla extract and rose water, and stir gently until all are well incorporated. Next you can sift the flour, bicarbonate of soda and baking powder onto the mix, before folding in gently.

Divide the mixture between the 6 loaf cases and bake in the middle of the preheated oven for 15-20 minutes, or until a skewer inserted into the centre of a loaf comes out clean.

Let's get ready to drizzle
While the loaves are baking, you can make the pretty icing. Simply put the icing sugar, beetroot juice and rose water into a bowl and mix well. And that's it. It couldn't be easier.

Finished with petals
When the loaves are cooked, allow them to cool before drizzling with the icing mix and sprinkling with rose petals. It's an English summer's day on a plate, and I believe has the power to conjure up the feeling of sunshine even when it's raining outside.

Inspired by an **ENGLISH COUNTRY GARDEN,**
this is the perfect accompaniment to cucumber
sandwiches on the croquet lawn surrounded by

rose beds & dancing butterflies.

Traditionally, a French wedding breakfast includes a DELICIOUS STRAWBERRY SOUP *with* **borage, a pretty cucumber-flavoured herb** *also known as starflower. This inspired me to create* this delicious summery sponge cake.

Cucumber & strawberry cake

Serves 6-8

100g	cucumber
100g	strawberries
1 tsp	vanilla extract
125g	caster sugar
100g	unsalted butter (at room temperature)
2	large free-range eggs
150g	self-raising flour
½ tsp	baking powder

Filling

100g	icing sugar
50g	unsalted butter (at room temperature)
1 tsp	vanilla extract
	a few strawberries

Preheat the oven to 180°C/350°F/Gas Mark 4.
Line 2 x 15cm round loose-bottomed sandwich tins with baking parchment.

Wash and finely grate the cucumber, then leave in a sieve to drain – cucumber is 98% water. If you like, why not save the cucumber juice – it's rich in vitamin C, has antioxidant skin-soothing properties, and makes a refreshing drink or cooling facial treatment.

Place the strawberries, vanilla extract and 15g of the caster sugar into a blender and blitz until you have a smooth puree.

In a separate bowl, cream together the remaining sugar and softened butter until light and fluffy. Now crack the eggs into another bowl and break up with a fork. Gradually add the eggs to the sugar and butter mix, beating as you do to ensure everything is nicely combined. Try not to add the eggs too quickly, or the mixture may curdle. If it does start to curdle, keep beating and add a tablespoon or two of flour to bring it back, then continue adding the egg.

Now you can add the grated cucumber, folding in gently. Sift the flour and baking powder onto the mix, and fold in gently. Add your strawberry puree next and, you've guessed it, fold in gently.

Divide your mixture between the two tins and bake on the middle shelf of the preheated oven for 15-20 minutes, until a skewer inserted into the centre of a cake comes out clean. Allow the cakes to cool on a cooling rack before you remove the tins.

Let's get filling

Place the softened butter, icing sugar and vanilla extract in a bowl and whisk until light and fluffy. Smooth the filling onto the top of one cake. Slice the strawberries and place around the edge, before placing the other cake on top.

To decorate, add a light dusting of sugar and a few sliced strawberries, and that's all it needs. Perfect for a wedding, or as a sweet treat packed with strawberry sunshine.

Fennel & orange upside-down cake

Serves 6-8

1	fennel bulb
3	unwaxed oranges – juice, zest & slices
10g	demerara sugar
55g	unsalted butter (at room temperature)
225g	caster sugar
3	medium free-range eggs (separated)
120g	self-raising flour
1 tsp	baking powder

Preheat the oven to 180°C/350°F/Gas Mark 4.
Line a 20cm round loose-bottomed tin with baking parchment.

Wash and finely slice the fennel bulb. Wash and zest all three oranges. Juice two. Cut the pith off the third orange and finely slice.

Sprinkle the demerara sugar over the base of the lined tin, then carefully arrange the fennel and orange slices – these will become the decoration on top of your cake. Cream the softened butter and caster sugar together.

Separate the eggs and add the yolks to the caster sugar, whisking all the time until the mixture is light and fluffy. Now mix in the orange juice and zest, ensuring everything is nicely combined. Sift the flour and baking powder onto the mix and fold in.

Whisk the egg whites until stiff, then fold gently into the mixture.

Carefully spoon the mixture into the cake tin, on top of the fennel and orange slices, then place in the middle of the preheated oven to bake for 25-35 minutes. Check it's cooked by inserting a skewer into the centre of the cake, if it comes out clean, the cake's baked.

Leave on a cooling rack and when cool, cover with a plate and turn upside down, carefully removing the tin to leave the orange and fennel slices on top of the cake.

Refreshing fennel

Add some ORANGE PEEL & ANY REMAINING SLICED FENNEL *to some boiling water, leave it to steep for 4 minutes and you'll have*

a refreshing orange & fennel tea.

The perfect accompaniment for your cake.

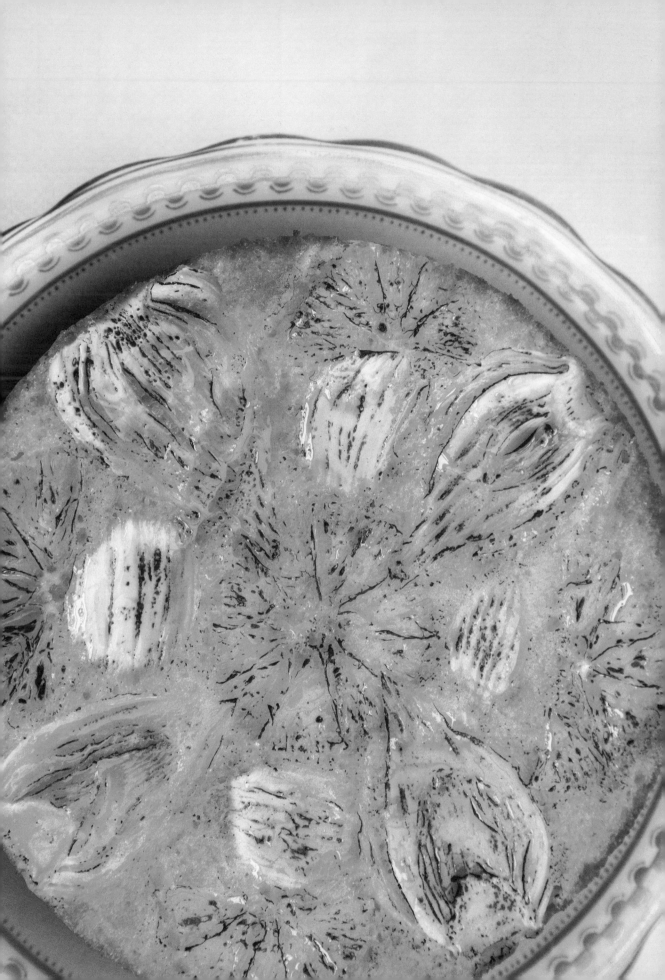

Fennel & pear tarts

Makes 6 tarts

1	fennel bulb
3	pears
250g	puff pastry (ready-made is just fine)
25g	unsalted butter (at room temperature)
25g	soft brown sugar
6	star anise

**Preheat the oven to 200°C/400°F/Gas Mark 6.
Line a large baking tray with baking parchment.**

Wash and finely slice the fennel bulb. Wash, core and finely slice the pears.

Roll out the puff pastry and cut out 6 x 10cm circles. Score each circle 1cm from the edge, place onto a baking tray then prick with a fork.

In a separate bowl, cream the butter and sugar together. Spread a little (reserving some to spread on top) over each of the pastry circles. Now you're ready to divide the sliced pears and fennel between the 6 circles, arranging each in a fan.

Brush the pear and fennel with the reserved butter and sugar mixture, place a star anise on top of each tart, then pop into the middle of the preheated oven to bake for 15-20 minutes, until the pastry has risen and is a lovely golden colour.

Remove from the oven once cooked and enjoy warm, or cold, both are equally delicious.

Fennel & chocolate torte

Serves 6-8

1	fennel bulb
12	large dark chocolate callets
175g	unsalted butter (at room temperature)
175g	soft brown sugar
3	large free-range eggs
150g	self-raising flour
3 tbsp	cocoa powder
8 tbsp	milk (any kind is fine)

Preheat the oven to 180°C/350°F/Gas Mark 4.
Line a 20cm round loose-bottomed tin with baking parchment.

Wash and finely slice the fennel bulb. Arrange the fennel slices on the base of the lined tin and sprinkle the chocolate callets into the gaps. In a large bowl, cream the softened butter and sugar together until light and fluffy. Beat the eggs together in a jug before slowly adding them to the butter and sugar mixture, beating well between each addition.

Sieve the flour and cocoa powder onto the mixture and gently fold in, before gradually adding the milk, folding in as you do. Spoon the mixture into the cake tin, taking care not to disturb the carefully arranged fennel slices. Pop into the middle of the preheated oven and bake for 30-40 minutes, until a skewer inserted into the centre comes out clean.

Once ready, move to a cooling rack and leave to cool for 10 minutes. Cover the tin with a serving plate and turn upside down, carefully remove the tin revealing the fennel slices on top. Now just leave on the plate to finish cooling, or for as long as you can keep tempted fingers away.

This looks lovely as it is, but for added impact, try adding some candied fennel and a drizzle of melted chocolate. Delicious.

Bulging with flavour

Fennel has a sweet flavour that resembles

ANISE & LIQUORICE, *the leaves having a stronger taste than the bulb. It's also a rich source of vitamins and dietary fibre.*

Jerusalem artichoke, mango & lime sponge

Serves 6-8

200g	Jerusalem artichoke
150g	unsalted butter (at room temperature)
150g	caster sugar
3	medium free-range eggs
2 tsp	vanilla extract
200g	self-raising flour

Filling & drizzle decoration

2	unwaxed limes – juice & zest
1	mango
150ml	whipping cream

Preheat the oven to 180°C/350°F/Gas Mark 4.
Line 2 x 15cm round loose-bottomed sandwich tins with baking parchment.

Peel and finely grate the Jerusalem artichoke, taking care to watch your fingers as you do!

In a large bowl, cream together the softened butter and sugar. Add the eggs one at a time, beating into the mix. Now gradually add the grated artichoke and vanilla extract, ensuring all the ingredients are evenly combined. Then sift the flour on top, folding in gently to ensure everything is thoroughly mixed.

Pour the mixture evenly into the prepared tins and pop into the middle of the preheated oven for 25-35 minutes, until a skewer inserted into the centre of a cake comes out clean. Leave on a cooling rack for 10 minutes before removing from the tins, then leave to cool fully before decorating.

Now for the filling & decoration
Wash, zest and juice the limes, placing the zest and juice in separate bowls. Peel the mango and remove the stone. Cut one half of the mango into small cubes and add half of the lime zest.

For the cake drizzle, place the remaining half of the mango into a bowl and puree until smooth with a hand blender – the consistency should be pourable, but not runny. If it's too thick, add some lime juice, one teaspoon at a time, until it's pourable.

For the filling, pour the cream and remaining lime juice into a bowl, whip until it forms soft peaks, then fold in the rest of the lime zest.

Building your masterpiece
Spread the whipped cream filling on one sponge, then place the other sponge on top. Dust the top with icing sugar, add your mango cubes and lime zest, then finish with your mango cake drizzle. And now you're ready for your 'ta da!' moment.

Jerusalem artichoke & pomegranate cake

Serves 6-8

150g	Jerusalem artichoke
50g	unsalted butter (at room temperature)
100g	runny honey
2	medium free-range eggs
1 tsp	vanilla extract
150g	self-raising flour
1 tsp	baking powder
50g	ground almonds

Decoration

50g	icing sugar or xylitol icing sugar (see below)
2 tsp	pomegranate juice
150g	pomegranate seeds

Preheat the oven to 180°C/350°F/Gas Mark 4.
Line a 20cm round loose-bottomed tin with baking parchment.

Peel and finely grate the Jerusalem artichoke. Cream the butter and honey together.
Now crack the eggs into a bowl and break up with a fork, before gradually adding, while
still beating, to the butter and honey mix. Now add the grated artichoke and vanilla
extract and fold in gently.

Sift the flour, baking powder and ground almonds on top of your mixture and fold in gently,
making sure all the ingredients are well mixed.

Pour the mixture evenly into the prepared tin and place in the middle of the preheated oven
for 25-35 minutes, until a skewer inserted into the centre of the cake comes out clean. Move
to a cooling rack and leave for 10 minutes.

The icing on the cake

If you want to keep this cake refined sugar-free, use xylitol as the icing sugar – just blitz it in
a blender, or food processor, on high until it looks like icing sugar, it doesn't take long.

Put 50g of the pomegranate seeds into a blender (without the sugar/xylitol) and pulse a few
times, so the seeds break and release their juice. Use a seive to separate the juice from the
pulp, squeezing the last drops of juice from the pulp with the back of a spoon. Every drop
counts. Discard the spent pulp.

Add 2 teaspoons of the pomegranate juice to the icing sugar, adding more if you need it, and
mix until you have a smooth paste. Pour the icing over the cold cake, allowing it to drizzle
down the sides. Decorate with the remaining pomegranate seeds.

Kale marble cake

Serves 8-10

100g	kale
100g	beetroot (fresh or vacuum packed, just not pickled!)
50g	raspberries
150g	caster sugar
140ml	sunflower oil
2	medium free-range eggs
240g	self-raising flour
½ tsp	baking powder

Preheat the oven to 180°C/350°F/Gas Mark 4.
Line a 20cm loose-bottomed cake tin with baking parchment.

Wash and steam the kale until soft, then puree with a blender or food processor until smooth. Place the beetroot and raspberries into another mixing bowl and puree until silky. If you're using fresh beetroot, peel and halve the beetroot before steaming or roasting until soft (about 20 minutes).

Whisk the sugar, oil and eggs until light and fluffy. Sift the flour and baking powder on top, then fold in gently until all the ingredients are thoroughly combined. Now you're ready to split the mix in two, transferring one half to a clean bowl.

Add the kale puree to one half of the mixture and fold in gently, until nicely combined. In the other half, fold in the beetroot and raspberry puree.

Now take turns to add spoonfuls of each mixture to the baking tin. Bake for 30-40 minutes in the middle of the preheated oven, or until a skewer inserted into the centre of the cake comes out clean. Place on a cooling rack for 10 minutes, then lift out of the tin and leave to finish cooling.

I love to SURPRISE PEOPLE
with a slice of this cake.
From the outside, you can't tell what swirly secrets are hidden inside.
And it tastes even better than it looks.

Kale Swiss roll

Serves 6-8

Roll

100g	kale
70g	caster sugar
3	medium free-range eggs
70g	self-raising flour

Filling

80g	unsalted butter (at room temperature)
175g	icing sugar
1 tsp	vanilla extract
6 tbsp	jam (see pages 24 and 162)

Preheat the oven to 200°C/400°F/Gas Mark 6.
Line a 33cm x 23cm Swiss roll tin with baking parchment.

Wash and steam the kale until soft, then blitz in a food processor or with a hand blender until smooth. Set aside to cool.

Whisk the sugar and eggs together until light and fluffy. Now, making sure it's cool, you're ready to fold in the kale puree for that wonderful green colour. Sift the flour on top, then gently fold in, making sure everything is nicely combined.

Pour evenly into your prepared Swiss roll tin, and pop into the middle of the preheated oven to bake for 8-10 minutes, until a skewer inserted into the centre of your cake comes out clean.

When it's ready, carefully turn the cake out of the tin onto a lightly sugared piece of greaseproof paper. Peel off the baking parchment and neaten the edges with a quick trim, if needed. Allow to cool for 3 minutes – just don't let it go cold or it'll be difficult to roll.

Score one short side with a sharp knife, about 1cm in from the edge. Then, using the greaseproof paper, roll up from the scored side. Rest it, with the seam on the bottom, to finish cooling.

Now for the filling
Cream the butter, icing sugar and vanilla extract in a bowl until light and fluffy. Make the jam of your choice.

The final stage, building your Swiss roll
Unroll the sponge and using a palette knife, spread the buttercream evenly over the inner surface, then spread the jam carefully on top. Using the greaseproof paper, roll the sponge back up, placing it seam-side down again.

A light dusting of icing sugar is the finishing touch, and this beautiful bright green roll is good to go.

Kale & beetroot chocolate cake

Two of your superfoods, and two from the vegetable colour chart, in one cake – this is already a winner. Kale's excellent fibre content makes it great for aiding digestion and elimination. It's nutrient-rich and packed with beneficial vitamins, folate and magnesium.

Serves 6-8

200g	beetroot (fresh or vacuum packed, just not pickled!)
100g	kale
50ml	water
85g	dark chocolate (70% minimum cocoa solids)
140g	light brown sugar
30g	caster sugar
125ml	sunflower oil
1 tsp	vanilla extract
200g	self-raising flour
30g	cocoa powder
1 tsp	baking powder

Filling

30g	non-dairy butter (to keep this cake vegan)
100g	icing sugar
2 tsp	beetroot juice

Preheat the oven to 180°C/350°F/Gas Mark 4.
Line 2 x 18cm round loose-bottomed sandwich tins with baking parchment.

If you're using fresh beetroot, wash, halve and roast for about 20 minutes, until soft. If you're using vacuum packed, you can skip this step.

Wash and steam the kale for 5 minutes until soft, then place in a large bowl with the beetroot and water, and puree until smooth with a food processor or hand blender. Add the chocolate, broken into small chunks, while the mix is still warm to allow the chocolate to melt in.

In a separate bowl, whisk together the sugars, oil and vanilla extract. Once the chocolate has melted into the kale and beetroot mixture, stir this into the vanilla cream. Now sift the flour, cocoa powder and baking powder directly onto the mixture and fold in, making sure all the ingredients are evenly combined.

Divide the mixture between your two lined tins and bake on the middle shelf of the preheated oven for 45 minutes, until a skewer inserted into the centre of a cake comes out clean. Place on a cooling rack for 10 minutes before lifting out of the tins.

Let's get filling

Cream the butter and icing sugar together. Depending on which dairy-free butter you're using, you may need to add a little more icing sugar to get a light and fluffy filling. Now just stir in the beetroot juice, and you're ready to smooth it over the bottom half of your cake. Place the second sponge on top and finish with a twist or two of candied beetroot. Simple. Perfect. Delicious.

Marrow & apple butter

Marrow

Makes 400g
450g	marrow
225g	apples
85g	maple syrup
2 tsp	cinnamon

400g sterilised jam jar or Kilner jar.

Peel, deseed and cut the marrow into chunks. Peel, core and cut the apples into chunks. Place in a saucepan with the maple syrup and cinnamon, bring to the boil, then reduce to a simmer, stirring occasionally, until all the ingredients are nice and soft. This usually takes about 35 minutes.

Now just puree until smooth with a hand blender or food processor, then spoon into the sterilised jar. The butter will keep for up to a week in the fridge.

This is lovely spread thickly on hot cross buns, or even just a nice simple doorstep of toast.

If you don't have marrow, you could try
PARSNIP, PEAR & NUTMEG
as a tasty alternative.

Marrow & banana muffins

Makes 6 muffins

200g	marrow
130g	caster sugar
85g	unsalted butter (at room temperature)
1½ tsp	vanilla extract
2	medium free-range eggs
2	ripe bananas
80g	wholemeal self-raising flour
80g	self-raising flour
1 tsp	baking powder

Buttercream icing

60g	unsalted butter (at room temperature)
140g	icing sugar
1	banana or banana chips

Preheat the oven to 180°C/350°F/Gas Mark 4.
Place 6 muffin cases into a muffin tin.

Peel, deseed and finely grate the marrow. Cream the sugar, butter and vanilla extract together until light and fluffy. Now you're ready to add the eggs, one at a time, beating the mixture as you do.

Peel and mash the banana, then beat this into the mixture. Now add the grated marrow and gently fold in. Sift the two flours and baking powder on top, then gently fold into the mixture, taking care to make sure it's all nicely combined.

Pour the mixture equally into the muffin cases and pop into the middle of the preheated oven to bake for 15 minutes, or until a skewer inserted into a muffin comes out clean. Leave to one side on a baking rack to cool completely before decorating.

The finishing touch
Cream the softened butter and icing sugar until light and fluffy. Once the cakes are fully cooled, decorate with the buttercream icing and slices of banana.

This is a great recipe to make with children, the muffins are simple to make and decorate, and they look fantastic.

Marrow & gooseberry tart

Makes 6 slices

200g	marrow
200g	gooseberries
2	medium free-range egg whites (at room temperature)
80g	caster sugar
batch	sweet potato shortcrust pastry (see page 190)

Preheat the oven to 180°C/350°F/Gas Mark 4.
Grease a 35cm x 10cm x 2½cm loose-bottomed rectangular flan pan.
You'll also need baking beans and parchment.

Prepare the pastry first, see my recipe on page 190. Wrap it in cling film and chill in the fridge for an hour before using.

After the pastry has chilled, roll it out to ½cm thick and line the tin, making sure to push it into the edges and corners. Prick the base all over with a fork. Line with baking parchment and beans, and pop into the middle of the preheated oven to bake for 10 minutes. Once baked, take out and reduce the oven temperature to 160°C/325°F/Gas Mark 3.

Peel, deseed and dice the marrow. Wash the gooseberries and dry with kitchen towel.

Whisk the egg whites and sugar until nicely combined. Fold in the grated marrow and gooseberries. Now you're ready to spoon the mixture evenly into your pastry-lined tin.

Pop into the middle of the oven and bake for 40-50 minutes. This is delicious eaten warm or cold. Just don't leave it too long. This tangy tart needs to be eaten on the day of cooking to be enjoyed at its best, which has never been a problem in my house.

The gooseberry is no mere fool

It's odd that the UNDERRATED GOOSEBERRY
*isn't used **more in the culinary world,** it has such a*

DELICIOUS ZESTY FLAVOUR, yet is mostly only used in a gooseberry fool.

Marrow & pine nut cake

I think this cake should really be called a cloud cake, it's so soft, fluffy and delicate.

Serves 6-8

200g	marrow
100g	agave syrup
3	medium free-range eggs
150g	ground almonds
30g	gluten-free plain flour
1 tsp	baking powder
20g	pine nuts

Preheat the oven to 180°C/350°F/Gas Mark 4.
Line a 20cm round springform tin with baking parchment.

Peel, deseed and finely grate the marrow. You may find it easier to cut the marrow into chunks to grate it.

Whisk the agave syrup and eggs together until light and fluffy. Fold in the grated marrow. Sift the ground almonds, flour and baking powder on top, then gently fold in, making sure everything is thoroughly combined.

Pour the mixture evenly into the prepared tin, sprinkle generously with the pine nuts, then pop into the middle of the preheated oven to bake for 35-45 minutes, until a skewer inserted into the centre of the cake comes out clean. Leave on a cooling rack for 10 minutes before taking out of the tin.

This easy to make, even easier to eat cake is now ready.

Size matters

While undoubtedly impressive, huge marrows are best saved for gardening competitions – they get more watery and bitter the larger they grow. USE THE SMALLEST MARROW YOU CAN FIND, *ideally no bigger than your forearm, for this lovely light cake. Other vegetables that work well include* PARSNIPS, COURGETTES & BUTTERNUT SQUASH.

Parsnip & carrot Christmas cake

This fabulous family Christmas cake can be made well in advance, and tastes great if you keep 'feeding' it with brandy.

Serves 10-12

150g	parsnips	1	unwaxed orange – juice & zest
150g	carrots	250g	unsalted butter (at room temperature)
350g	sultanas	300g	dark brown sugar
350g	raisins	5	medium free-range eggs
350g	currants	350g	plain flour
100g	mixed cherries	1 tsp	mixed spice
100g	mixed nuts	½ tsp	ground clove
150ml	brandy	1 tsp	ground cinnamon

Preheat the oven to 150°C/300°F/Gas Mark 2.
Line a 20cm loose-bottomed cake tin with baking parchment.

Place the sultanas, raisins, currants, mixed cherries, mixed nuts, brandy, orange juice and zest in a large mixing bowl, stir well, then cover and leave to soak overnight.

The next day, peel and grate the carrots and parsnips. In a separate bowl, cream together the butter and sugar. Crack the eggs into a jug and break up with a fork, before adding to the buttercream, beating after each addition of egg to ensure a nice lump-free consistency.

Now you're ready to stir in the soaked fruit mixture, followed by the grated carrot and parsnip. Finally sift the flour and spices on top, stirring well to ensure everything is evenly mixed.

Spoon the mixture into the prepared tin and pop into the preheated oven to bake for 120-150 minutes, or until a skewer inserted into the middle of the cake comes out clean. For the last 30 minutes of baking, you may want to loosely cover your cake with baking parchment, to prevent it from browning too much, just keep an eye on it as it bakes. Move to a cooling rack when ready and allow to cool before removing from the tin.

'Feeding' your cake.

You can enjoy your cake straight away, but I like to 'feed' it for a few months first. Wrap your cake in it baking parchment and store it in a cool dry place until Christmas, or when required. Once a month, unwrap the parchment, prick the cake in several places with a skewer, drizzle some brandy over the holes, then wrap it up again until the following month. This will give you a wonderfully moist, slightly boozy, very delicious and moreish cake.

This cake looks great served just as it is, or you can cover it with marzipan and icing, to create a blank canvas for your Christmas centrepiece.

Parsnips taste even better when they've been exposed, while still in the ground, to THE FIRST FROST. **The frost changes the starches to sugar,** *giving the parsnip its* UNIQUE FLAVOUR & SWEETNESS.

Parsnip & honey scones

Makes 6 scones

150g	parsnips
140g	unsalted butter (at room temperature)
30g	caster sugar
70g	runny honey
1	medium free-range egg
425g	self-raising flour
1 tsp	baking powder
½ tsp	grated nutmeg
1 tbsp	milk (any kind is fine)

Preheat the oven to 170°C/325°F/Gas Mark 3.
Line a baking tray with baking parchment, you'll also need a 7cm round cutter.

Peel and finely grate the parsnips. In a separate bowl, cream the butter and sugar together until light and fluffy. Now add the honey and egg, mixing well to ensure all the ingredients are nicely combined. Add the grated parsnip and mix in well.

Sift the flour, baking powder and ground nutmeg onto your parsnip mixture and mix in well. Keep mixing until it forms a soft dough.

Place the dough onto a lightly floured surface and flatten with the palm of your hand, to a depth of about 2cm. Now cut out your scones, reworking the dough when it's full of holes, until it's all used up. If the last bit's too small to make a whole scone, I like to create a fun shape and cook it as it is.

Place the scones onto the prepared baking tray, brush with milk to glaze, then place in the middle of the preheated oven to bake for 10-15 minutes, until the scones have a lovely golden brown colour. To check if the scones are cooked, tap one on its bottom. If it sounds hollow, it's ready. If it doesn't, bake for a few minutes more.

When they're ready, take out of the oven and place on a cooling rack for 10 minutes, before taking out of the tin.

These are delicious eaten warm, and go perfectly with sweetcorn lemon curd, see page 200. They're also ideal for making in advance and can be frozen.

Parsnip walnut streusel cake

Serves 8-10

150g	parsnips
1	medium free-range egg
140ml	sunflower oil
140g	caster sugar
140g	self-raising flour
1 tsp	allspice
1 tsp	baking powder

Streusel topping

50g	unsalted butter (at room temperature)
75g	dark brown sugar
100g	wholemeal flour
80g	walnut pieces

Preheat the oven to 180°C/350°F/Gas Mark 4.
Line an 18cm round cake tin with baking parchment.

Starting at the top

We begin with the topping. Rub the butter, sugar and flour together until it looks like breadcrumbs, add the walnut pieces, then place in a fridge while you make the cake.

Let's get to the bottom of this

Now you're ready to make the cake. Peel and finely grate the parsnips. In a separate bowl, whisk the egg, sunflower oil and sugar together, then add the grated parsnip and fold in gently to keep in all the air you've just whisked in. Now sift the flour, allspice and baking powder on top, before carefully folding into the parsnip and egg mix, making sure everything is nicely combined.

Pour evenly into the prepared tin. Now you're ready for your streusel topping that's been chilling in the fridge. Sprinkle evenly over the top of the mixture, pop into the middle of the preheated oven and bake for 40 minutes, until a skewer inserted into the centre of the cake comes out clean. Place on a cooling rack and leave for 10 minutes before removing from the tin.

While the cake is believed to originate in either Germany or France, the German name STREUSEL *means*

'something scattered or sprinkled',

it's very similar to the English verb 'strew'.

Parsnip & fig squares

Makes 12 squares

150g	parsnips
100g	agave nectar
2	medium free-range eggs
120g	self-raising flour
1 tsp	coriander powder
1 tsp	baking powder
4	ripe figs

Preheat the oven to 180°C/350°F/Gas Mark 4.
Line a 20cm x 20cm square tin with baking parchment.

Peel and finely grate the parsnips – keeping fingers away from the sharp surface.

Whisk the agave nectar and eggs in a large bowl until light and fluffy. Add the grated parsnips and fold in gently. Into the same bowl, sift the flour, baking powder and coriander, then gently fold into the mix.

Pour into the prepared tin and decorate with slices of fig. Bake in the middle of the preheated oven for 15-20 minutes, until a skewer inserted into the centre comes out clean. Place on a cooling rack and remove from the tin after about 10 minutes.

One lump or two?

In Europe, before sugar was widely available to all, and a luxury only a few could afford, parsnips would be finely ground and used to sweeten jams and cakes. I'm not sure what they added to their tea though.

Parsnip nut crumble Bundts

Makes 6 mini Bundts

250g	parsnips
250g	unsalted butter (at room temperature)
200g	caster sugar
4	medium free-range eggs
200g	self-raising flour
25g	demerara sugar
1 tsp	mixed spice
25g	mixed nuts

Preheat the oven to 190°C/375°F/Gas Mark 5.
Grease and flour 6 mini Bundt tins.

Peel and finely grate the parsnips. Cream the softened butter and sugar together until light and fluffy. Now add the eggs one at a time and beat in well, before stirring in the grated parsnip. Sift the flour and mixed spice onto the parsnip mix, then fold in gently, making sure everything is thoroughly combined.

Creating your crumble
In a separate bowl, mix together the demerara sugar, mixed spice and mixed nuts, to make your crumble.

Prepare to bake
Divide the nut crumble evenly between the Bundt tins. Give the tins a gentle shake to make sure the nut crumble covers the base. Now divide your parsnip batter evenly between the tins, pouring on top of the crumble. Place in the middle of the preheated oven and bake for 15-20 minutes, until the Bundts have risen and are firm to the touch.

Remove from the oven once baked and place on a cooling rack for 10 minutes, before carefully taking out of the tins.

During World War II in Britain,
when fruit wasn't widely available,
mock bananas were made from parsnips
– they share the same sweet spiciness,
but I can't think they fooled anybody.

Parsnip & toffee apple loaf

Serves 8-10

150g	parsnips
1	apple
150g	unsalted butter (at room temperature)
150g	caster sugar
3	medium free-range eggs
4 tbsp	apple juice
200g	self-raising flour

Toffee apple topping

30g	unsalted butter
150g	soft brown sugar
150ml	double cream (or your preferred non-dairy alternative)
1	apple

Preheat the oven to 170°C/325°F/Gas Mark 3.
Line a 900g loaf tin with baking parchment.

Peel and finely grate the parsnips, wash and coarsely grate the apple. Then, in a large bowl, cream the butter and sugar until light and fluffy.

Crack the eggs into a separate bowl and break up with a fork. Now pour the eggs gradually into the creamed butter and sugar, beating continually to ensure a nice smooth texture.

Add the grated parsnip and apple to the mixture, stirring to ensure all the ingredients are nicely combined. Add the apple juice and stir in gently. Sift the flour directly onto the mix and fold in gently, until everything is thoroughly combined.

Spoon the mixture into the lined tin and place on the middle shelf of the preheated oven to bake for 40-50 minutes. Check after 30 minutes to see how the loaf is browning. If necessary, cover with a piece of baking parchment for the remaining time. When a skewer inserted into the centre of the loaf comes out clean, your loaf is cooked. Move to a cooling rack and leave for 15 minutes before removing from the tin.

Toffee apple topping

Heat the butter and sugar in a saucepan over a medium heat and gradually bring to the boil, stirring continuously. Boil for 5 minutes, until it's a golden colour, this time without stirring. Remove from the heat and stir in the cream. Peel and chop the apple into cubes, add to the mixture and mix in well, then leave to cool.

When the loaf has cooled, pour the toffee apple sauce over the top and serve.

Pea, mint & chocolate cake

The inspiration for this cake came to me as I was eating a mint chocolate at the end of a meal that had also included minted peas, and hey presto – Pea, mint and chocolate cake.

Serves 6-8

170g	peas (fresh or frozen, garden or petits pois, all are fine)
2 tsp	vanilla extract
120ml	milk (semi-skimmed or full fat is best)
2 tsp	lemon juice
125ml	sunflower oil
2	medium free-range eggs
120g	caster sugar
200g	self-raising flour
3 tsp	cocoa powder
1 tsp	baking powder

Filling

60g	unsalted butter (at room temperature)
200g	icing sugar
1 tbsp	cocoa powder
1 tsp	mint flavouring
2 tbsp	water

Preheat the oven to 180°C/350°F/Gas Mark 4.
Line 2 x 18cm sandwich tins with baking parchment.

Steam the peas until soft. Cool with a splash of cold water, then add the vanilla extract and milk and blitz with a hand blender, or food processor, until smooth. Stir in the lemon juice.

In a separate bowl, whisk the sunflower oil, eggs and sugar together until light and fluffy, then fold into the pea puree. Now sift the flour, cocoa powder and baking powder onto the mixture, and fold in gently until all the ingredients are nicely combined.

Pour the mixture evenly into the prepared tins and pop into the middle of the preheated oven to bake for 20-30 minutes, until a skewer inserted into the centre of the cake comes out clean. Place on a cooling rack for 10 minutes before removing the tin, then leave to cool completely before assembling.

Compiling your cake

Cream the softened butter, icing sugar and cocoa powder, then add the mint flavouring and water, creaming continually until light and fluffy. Now you're ready to compile your cake.

Spread the filling over the top of one cake, smoothing right up to the edges, then place the second cake on top. If your cake has risen too much, you can always cut the top off the lower sponge, so you have a nice flat surface for the filling.

A PEAS OF CAKE

It's fun to decorate the edge with peas, AND CROWN WITH A SPRING OF FRESH MINT.

Pea & mint ice cream

Makes 1 litre

300g	peas (fresh or frozen, garden or petits pois, all are fine)
40g	fresh mint
100ml	milk (any kind is fine)
2	medium free-range eggs
80g	caster sugar
200ml	double cream (or your preferred non-dairy alternative)

Use an ice cream maker, or make by hand in a clean 1 litre freezer-safe container.

Place the peas (defrost first if using frozen peas) and mint leaves into a bowl, add the milk then puree carefully, so you're not wearing the combination, until completely smooth.

Whisk the eggs together until light and fluffy, add half the sugar and whisk again, then add the other half and whisk until everything is evenly combined. Now gradually add the cream and whisk slowly, until this too is completely mixed in.

Stir your pea and mint puree into your egg and cream blend, then place into your ice cream maker and follow the maker's instructions.

If you're making by hand, transfer your mixture into a suitable freezer-safe container and place in the freezer for about 30 minutes, until the edges start to freeze. Take out and beat the mixture using a hand mixer or wooden spoon. By breaking up the ice cream, you're breaking up the ice crystals, which will make it smoother and creamier. Place back in the freezer and repeat after another 30 minutes, and possibly once more, until it looks and feels like ice cream.

Why not add some chocolate chips too, for a delicious mint and chocolate chip ice cream with a secret ingredient and added yummmm.

The garden pea has been around SINCE 4800 BC, ACCORDING TO ARCHAEOLOGISTS.

That's a big history for a little vegetable.

Pea, strawberry & basil chiffon cake

A chiffon cake is so light it almost floats, hence 'chiffon'. It was invented in the 1920s by an aptly named Los Angeles insurance salesman, Harry Baker. He kept the recipe a secret for 20 years, before selling it to a cake-mix conglomerate.

Serves 6-8

120g	peas (fresh or frozen, garden or petits pois, all are fine)
30g	strawberries
60ml	sunflower oil
150g	caster sugar
4	medium free-range egg yolks
6	medium free-range egg whites
115g	plain flour
20g	corn flour
1 tsp	baking powder

Filling

80g	unsalted butter (at room temperature)
300g	icing sugar
	couple of sprigs of basil leaves
40g	fresh strawberries
	Fresh strawberries and basil leaves to garnish

Preheat the oven to 160°C/325°F/Gas Mark 3.
Line 4 x 20 cm sandwich tins, bases only, with baking parchment. Don't grease the sides.

Puree the peas, strawberries and oil until smooth. In a separate bowl, whisk half the sugar and all 4 egg yolks until light and fluffy. In another bowl, whisk together the remaining caster sugar with the egg whites until you have soft peaks.

Going back to the pea and strawberry puree, fold in the egg yolk mixture, then sift the flour, corn flour and baking powder on top and fold in. Keep folding, this time it's a quarter of the whisked egg whites to loosen the mixture, then fold in the rest of the egg whites. Folding in gently will retain the air you whisked in, which helps to give this cake its incredible lightness.

Pour the mixture evenly into your prepared tins. Place in the middle of the preheated oven and bake for 20-25 minutes, until a skewer inserted into the centre of a cake comes out clean.

Immediately on taking the cakes out of the oven, run a knife or metal spatula around each cake and turn upside down onto a cooling rack. Leave for 5 minutes before taking out of the tins. Don't let them cool down in the tin for too long, or any trapped steam will deflate the cake.

Fill me up

To make the two fillings, start by creaming the softened butter and icing sugar until light and fluffy.

Green basil filling. Puree the basil leaves, with a couple of tablespoons of the icing mixture, with a hand blender. Now add half of the icing mixture and fold into the basil puree.

Pink strawberry filling. In a separate bowl, use the cleaned hand blender to puree the strawberries. Take the remaining icing mixture and add fold in the pureed strawberries.

Stacked with scrumptiousness
Smooth the basil filling across the tops of two cakes, and the strawberry icing on the other two,
then layer alternately to create a chiffon cake tower. Decorate with strawberries and basil leaves.

This delicate cake needs to be enjoyed on the day of baking, it's not nearly so good later on.

Red & orange pepper & nectarine cake

Serves 8-10

Compote

1	large red pepper
1	large orange pepper
2	nectarines
70g	caster sugar
2 tbsp	water

Pastry cream

1	large free-range egg
1	large free-range egg yolk
30g	cornflour
80g	caster sugar
500ml	milk
1 tsp	vanilla extract
25g	unsalted butter

Sponge base

90g	unsalted butter (at room temperature)
70g	caster sugar
3	large free-range egg yolks
90g	self-raising flour
90ml	milk (any kind is fine)
1 tsp	vanilla extract

Meringue topping

3	large free-range egg whites (at room temperature)
170g	caster sugar

Preheat the oven to 180°C/350°F/Gas Mark 4.
Line a 23cm round springform tin with baking parchment.

Let's commence with the compote

Wash and halve the peppers, deseed and finely dice. Do the same with the nectarines. Heat the water and sugar in a saucepan until the sugar has dissolved. Add the peppers and simmer for 10 minutes, then add the nectarines and continue simmering until everything has softened and the water has been absorbed. Set aside to cool.

Next, comes the pastry cream

Whisk the egg and egg yolk with the cornflour and sugar. In a saucepan, heat the milk and vanilla extract until nearly boiling.

Now you're ready to whisk the milk into the egg mix. This is best done in thirds, whisking as you add the milk to ensure a smooth consistency. Once all the milk has been whisked in, pour the mixture back into the saucepan and bring to the boil, stirring continuously until it has thickened – you can tell it's ready when it coats the back of a wooden spoon. Finally, stir in the butter – the mixture is ready when it's smooth and shiny. Leave to one side to cool.

Now for the sponge base

Cream the butter and sugar in a large bowl. Add the egg yolks one at a time, beating between each addition. Sift the flour on top and fold in, then gradually fold in the milk and vanilla extract. When everything is nicely combined, gently tip the mixture into the prepared tin.

Bake on the middle shelf of the preheated oven for 15 minutes, or until a skewer inserted into the centre of the cake comes out clean. Leave on a cooling rack for 10 minutes before lifting out of the tin.

Finally, the meringue topping
Line the base of the sponge tin with baking parchment. In a clean dry bowl, whisk the egg whites until they form soft peaks. Gradually add the sugar, a tablespoon at a time, whisking all the time until it's firm. Spread the meringue over the base of the tin and pop into the middle of the preheated oven to bake for 30-40 minutes, until golden brown. Place on a cooling rack to cool.

Assembling your cake
Now for the easy and impressive bit. Once every component is cold, you can start assembling. Begin by placing the sponge on your chosen plate, cover generously with pastry cream, spoon on the compote – saving just a little, then crown with your meringue and the last of the compote.

Yellow pepper tropical fruit loaf

Serves 8-10

1	large yellow pepper
½	papaya
100g	unsalted butter (at room temperature)
100g	caster sugar
2	medium free-range eggs
150g	self-raising flour

Decoration

130ml	whipping cream
30ml	coconut cream
½	papaya
1	passion fruit

Preheat the oven to 180°C/350°F/Gas Mark 4.
Line a 900g loaf tin with baking parchment.

Wash, quarter and deseed the yellow pepper. To remove the skin, score it with a sharp knife, place it in a jug or bowl and cover with boiling water. Leave for 10-15 minutes, and you should be able to peel the skin off easily. Now just dice the pepper flesh. Peel, deseed and cut the papaya into small cubes.

In a separate bowl, cream together the butter and sugar. Crack the eggs into a bowl, break up with a fork then gradually add to the creamed butter and sugar, beating well between each addition. Fold in the diced papaya and yellow pepper. Sift the flour on top and fold in, making sure everything is thoroughly mixed.

Pour the mixture evenly into the prepared tin, then pop into the middle of the preheated oven to bake for 30-40 minutes, until a skewer inserted into the centre of the loaf comes out clean. Leave on a cooling rack for 10 minutes before taking out of the tin, then leave to cool completely before icing.

Let's get decorating

Whisk the cream and coconut cream until soft. Smooth generously over the top of the loaf.

Halve the passion fruit, scoop out the delicious seeds into a bowl. Peel, deseed and dice the papaya, then mix with the passion fruit. Sprinkle the fruit over the top of your loaf – you can add as much or as little as you want, or you can choose different tropical fruit, it's entirely up to you.

Potato, chocolate & orange muffins

Makes 8 muffins

300g	potatoes (Maris Piper are one of the best)
40g	unsalted butter
100g	dark chocolate (70% minimum cocoa solids)
1	unwaxed orange – juice & zest
50g	caster sugar
2	large free-range eggs

Choice of two toppings:

Avocado & chocolate icing (see page 14)

or

Dark chocolate topping

50g	dark chocolate (70% minimum cocoa solids)
1	unwaxed orange – juice & zest
100ml	double cream (or your preferred non-dairy alternative) some candied orange slices

Preheat the oven to 190°C/375°F/Gas Mark 5.
Line a muffin tray with cases.

Peel and steam the potatoes until soft, then mash until nice and smooth.

Place the butter and chocolate, broken into chunks, into a heatproof bowl and pop into the middle of the oven to melt while the oven preheats. Remove when the chocolate's melted and stir well.

In a large bowl, add the mashed potato, chocolate and butter. Stir well, before adding the orange juice and zest, and give another stir.

In a separate bowl, whisk together the sugar and eggs until light and fluffy, then gently fold in the chocolately mashed potato.

Spoon the mixture evenly between the muffin cases, pop into the middle of the preheated oven and bake for 15 minutes, until a skewer inserted into the centre of a muffin comes out clean. Leave on a cooling rack for 10 minutes before lifting the muffin cases from the tin, then allow to finish cooling before icing.

Crowning your magnificent muffins

Break the chocolate into a bowl. Bring the cream to the boil in a saucepan, then pour over the chocolate pieces to melt, stirring until you have a lovely smooth sauce. Mix in the orange juice and zest. When the mixture feels firm, pipe or spoon the icing over your cooled muffins. Add candied orange segments as a tasty finishing flourish, and they're ready to eat.

Potato & coconut jammy squares

Serves 6-8

125g	potatoes (Maris Piper are one of the best)
125g	unsalted butter (at room temperature)
100g	caster sugar
2	medium free-range eggs
6 tbsp	milk (any kind is fine)
3 tbsp	desiccated coconut
125g	self-raising flour
8 tbsp	jam (any flavour is fine, see pages 24 and 162)

Preheat the oven to 180°C/350°F/Gas Mark 4.
Line a 20cm x 20cm square tin with baking parchment.

Peel and steam the potatoes until soft, then drain and mash until smooth. Leave to one side to cool.

Cream the butter and sugar in a bowl until light and fluffy. Add the eggs, one at a time, and beat in well to retain the nice smooth texture. Now add the mashed potato, milk and 1 tablespoon of coconut, and gently fold in.

Sift the flour onto your mixture, then fold in gently until everything is nicely combined.

Pour half the mixture evenly into the prepared tin. Carefully spread the jam over the top, then pour the other half of the mixture over the jam. Sprinkle the top with the remaining coconut. Pop into the middle of the preheated oven to bake for 35 minutes, until the top feels firm when pressed.

Remove from the oven once cooked, place on cooling rack and leave to cool, or for as long as you can manage before tucking in – just mind that hot jammy centre!

GOOD OLD SPUDS

So often taken for granted, potatoes actually provide a significant amount of FIBRE, POTASSIUM, FOLATE, MAGNESIUM, COPPER *&* ZINC.

Potato & cappuccino loaf

Serves 8-10

150g	potatoes (Maris Piper are one of the best)
60g	dark chocolate (70% minimum cocoa solids)
3 tsp	instant coffee granules or a shot of espresso
4 tbsp	milk (any kind is fine)
150g	unsalted butter (at room temperature)
150g	caster sugar
3	large free-range eggs
150g	self-raising flour
20g	cocoa powder
1 tsp	baking powder

Topping

50g	unsalted butter
3 tbsp	milk (any kind is fine)
100g	white chocolate
175g	icing sugar

Preheat the oven to 180°C/350°F/Gas Mark 4.
Line a 900g loaf tin with baking parchment.

Peel and then boil the potatoes until soft, then drain and mash to a nice smooth lump-free texture.

While the oven's preheating, place a heatproof bowl with the chocolate, coffee and milk into the middle, and leave until the chocolate has melted. Carefully remove from the oven and stir well to combine all of the ingredients, then stir in the mashed potato.

In a separate bowl, cream the butter and sugar together until light and fluffy. Crack the eggs into a bowl and break up with a fork, then gradually add to the buttercream, beating in for a smooth consistency.

Next add the chocolate and potato mixture, folding in gently. And while you're doing so well at folding, sift the flour, cocoa powder and baking powder onto the cake mixture and gently fold in, making sure everything is nicely combined.

Pour the whole lot evenly into the prepared tin and pop into the middle of the preheated oven to bake for 30 minutes, until a skewer inserted into the centre of the loaf comes out clean. Leave on a cooling rack for 10 minutes before removing from the tin.

The crema on the coffee cake

Find a medium-sized bowl, or bain-marie if you have one, and add the butter, milk and white chocolate broken into chunks. Place your bowl over a saucepan of simmering water, making sure your bowl doesn't touch the water, and stir occasionally while your ingredients melt together.

Once nice and gooey, add the icing sugar and beat to a smooth paste. Now just spread it thickly over your cooled loaf, and finish with a dusting of cocoa powder. Delicious!

I like to serve a slab-sized slice with
A BIG MUG OF FROTHY COFFEE.
The potatoes add *a wonderful moisture*
and structure to the loaf.

Potato & stout cake

Serves 10-12

250g	potatoes (Maris Piper are one of the best)
400g	dried mixed fruit
50g	glacé cherries
200g	soft brown sugar
250ml	stout (such as Guinness or porter)
125g	unsalted butter
2	medium free-range eggs
1	unwaxed orange – juice & zest
385g	self-raising flour
2 tsp	mixed spice
½ tsp	baking powder

Preheat the oven to 180°C/350°F/Gas Mark 4.
Line a 23cm round loose-bottomed tin with baking parchment.

Start this very Irish influenced cake by soaking the mixed fruit, cherries and sugar in the stout, ideally overnight for best results. It's important to let your fruit soak, as dried fruit will take the moisture out of the cake when it cooks.

Peel and steam the potatoes until soft, then mash until nice and smooth. Add the butter, and when it's melted in, add the mixed fruit and stout mixture, stirring well to ensure everything is nicely combined.

Next you can add the eggs, orange juice and zest, and mix well. Then sift the flour, spices and baking powder on top, and stir well until thoroughly combined.

Pour the mixture evenly into the prepared tin and pop into the middle of the preheated oven to bake for 60 minutes, until a skewer inserted into the centre of the cake comes out clean. Remove from the oven and place on a cooling rack to cool completely before lifting out of the tin.

Max the moisture
For added moistness, prick the top of the cake in several places with a skewer while it's still warm, then pour 3 tablespoons of stout over your cake, before leaving to finish cooling.

No need to wait
Although it's recommended to let the cake rest for a day before cutting, it's just as delicious and moist the day it's made. Which is just as well, as I can never keep my family away from it for that long!

Pumpkin & apple treacle tarts

EF

Makes 12 tarts

Base

100g	unsalted butter (at room temperature)
25g	light brown sugar
170g	plain flour

Middle

200g	pumpkin
200g	apples
25g	caster sugar
50ml	water

Topping

200g	golden syrup
70g	porridge oats
1	unwaxed orange – juice & zest

Preheat the oven to 170°C/325°F/Gas Mark 3.
Grease a 12 hole loose-based mini sandwich tin.

Starting at the bottom of these tasty tarts, cream the brown sugar and butter together in a large bowl. Sift on the flour and mix until well combined.

Press the mixture into your prepared tin, using the back of a spoon or your fingertips to press down until firm, then finish by lightly pricking each base several times with a fork. Place into the preheated oven for 10 minutes, until baked and a nice golden colour. Leave on a cooling rack to one side.

Moving on to the middle

Peel and finely grate the pumpkin, then peel, core and coarsely grate the apple. In a saucepan over a medium heat, add the pumpkin, apple, caster sugar and water, stirring occasionally until the ingredients have gone soft and mushy. Spread the softened pumpkin and apple mix over the baked tart bases, covering well.

To the top!

Add the golden syrup, oats, orange juice and zest to a saucepan and warm over a medium heat, mixing well until the oats are well covered and the mixture is nicely combined. Spoon this carefully over the pumpkin and apple mix, spreading out evenly, before popping into the middle of the preheated oven to bake for 15 minutes, until pale and golden. Once ready, leave on a cooling rack, in the tin, until cold.

No need to hurry

Pumpkin and apple are a perfect combination, and these delicious tastes of autumn will keep for a week, ideal for making ahead of time. I love to go on a long country walk knowing I've these little tarts of perfection waiting for me to come back to.

Pumpkin & plum loaf

Serves 8-10

225g	pumpkin
2	ripe plums
120ml	sunflower oil
170g	soft brown sugar
2	medium free-range eggs
1	unwaxed orange – juice & zest
225g	self-raising flour
1½ tsp	bicarbonate of soda

Preheat the oven to 180°C/350°F/Gas Mark 4.
Line a 900g loaf tin with baking parchment.

Peel and finely grate the pumpkin, then wash, halve, stone and roughly chop the plums.

In a large bowl, whisk together the oil, sugar and eggs. Add the grated pumpkin, chopped plums, orange juice and zest, and mix well until all the ingredients are combined. Sift the flour and bicarbonate of soda onto the mixture, then carefully fold in, making sure everything is thoroughly combined.

Pour the mixture evenly into the prepared tin, then pop into the middle of the preheated oven to bake for 50 minutes, until a skewer inserted into the centre comes out clean. Place to one side on a cooling rack for 10 minutes before lifting out of the tin.

DID YOU KNOW...? *The name pumpkin* comes from the Greek word 'pepon' *meaning 'large melon'. Pumpkins are usually* HARVESTED IN OCTOBER, *but if none are available, you could try using another member of the gourd family, such as butternut squash, which works just as well and is available all year round.*

Pumpkin & parsnip Battenberg cake

History says that the Battenberg cake was created to celebrate the 1884 wedding of Prince Louis of Battenberg to Queen Victoria's granddaughter, Princess Victoria. But there are a few other stories too, so I can't be sure.

Serves 8

150g	pumpkin
150g	parsnips
2	medium free-range eggs
130g	caster sugar
120g	sunflower oil
240g	self-raising flour
½ tsp	baking powder

For the chocolate sponge

1 tbsp	cocoa powder
1 tbsp	milk (any kind is fine)

For the vanilla sponge

1 tsp	vanilla extract

To assemble

3 tbsp	apricot jam
500g	marzipan (ready-made is fine)

Preheat the oven to 180°C/350°F/Gas Mark 4.
Thoroughly grease a Battenberg tin.

Peel and finely grate the pumpkin and parsnips. Whisk the eggs, sugar and oil together until light and fluffy. Sift the flour and baking powder onto the eggs, then gently fold in.

Halve the mixture, transferring one half to a separate bowl – to make two sponges.

For the chocolate sponge – add the cocoa powder and milk to the mixture and fold in gently. Now add the grated pumpkin and fold in.

For the vanilla sponge – fold the vanilla extract and grated parsnip into the mixture.

Pour each mixture evenly into the prepared tin – 2 lines of chocolate and 2 lines of vanilla. Pop into the middle of the preheated oven to bake for 20-30 minutes, until a skewer inserted into the centre of a cake comes out clean. Place on a cooling rack for 10 minutes before taking out of the tin.

Building your Battenberg

A neatly made Battenberg cake is a technical challenge for any baker, so don't worry if your edges aren't perfect, it will still taste delicious.

Lightly dust some baking parchment with icing sugar, roll the marzipan out to an oblong, using the tin as a guide. You want the marzipan slightly longer than the cake and 4 times the width, roughly 25cm x 38cm, which will give you a little bit extra to play with.

The sponges should be fairly square, but if needed, slice the top off each cake to square up.

Warm the apricot jam in a small saucepan or the microwave. If it's lumpy, push it through a sieve. Brush the top of a vanilla and chocolate oblong with jam. Place a vanilla oblong on top of the chocolate. Now brush one side of the remaining chocolate oblong with jam, place beside the vanilla, on top of the other vanilla, then gently press them together. You should now have all four strips of sponge, stuck together to form a chequered square.

Brush jam over the marzipan. Now give the assembled cake a good push together, then carefully place it onto the marzipan. Using the baking parchment, slowly roll the cake over until the cake is encased and the marzipan joins together.

Now smooth the sides, using the paper to make sure that the marzipan has glued itself to the sponge. Finally, neaten your cake by cutting off any excess bits of marzipan with a sharp knife, and your cake fit for royalty is ready to serve. Enjoy!!

Pumpkin & butternut squash crisps & nibbles

SKIN CRISPS

Preheat the oven to 180°C/350°F/Gas Mark 4.

Spread your pumpkin and butternut squash skins evenly across a baking tray. Drizzle with some oil, not too much – you don't want to drown them.

To season, try a sprinkle of some herbs or spices of your choice, or a simple twist of salt and pepper.

Now pop into a preheated oven and bake for about 15 minutes, until golden and crunchy.

These are best eaten on the day of cooking, as they don't store very well.

SEED NIBBLES

Pumpkin seeds are a rich source of fibre and protein. They also contain exceptionally high levels of magnesium, which helps your body to absorb calcium.

Preheat the oven to 150°C/300°F/Gas Mark 2.

Wash the seeds in a colander to get rid of all the pulp. Spread them out on a baking tray, then simply pop them into the oven for about 30 minutes, just enough time for them to dry out and get nice and crunchy.

Take out of the oven and sprinkle with a sweet topping such as cinnamon, mixed spice or a drizzle of maple syrup, and just give them a stir. Or if you prefer a savoury snack, try sea salt, herbs or a spicy chilli topping.

Let your imagination run wild and try different toppings, or you can have them as they are, simply roasted.

These will keep for up to a week in an airtight container.

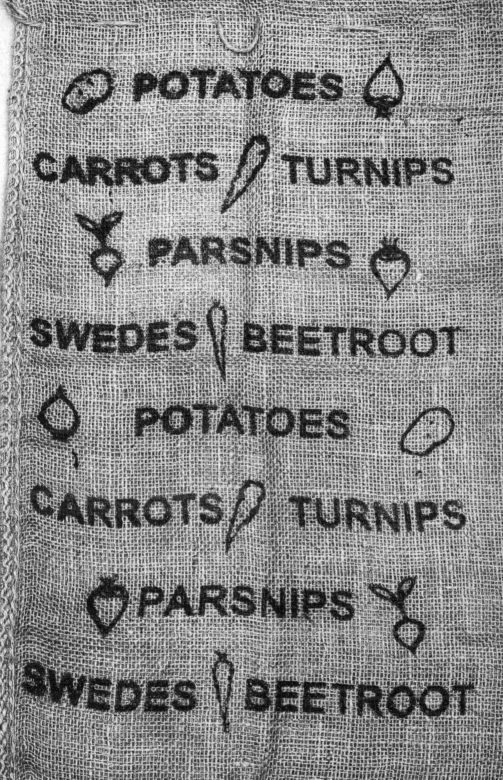

Perfect for the little people

This recipe also makes great

GINGERBREAD MEN & WOMEN

for a treat at Christmas time,

OR IN FACT, ANY TIME.

Pumpkin cookies

Makes 24 cookies

100g	pumpkin
60g	unsalted butter (at room temperature)
100g	light brown sugar
70g	black treacle
1	medium free-range egg
350g	plain flour
½ tsp	baking powder
3 tsp	ground ginger

Preheat the oven to 190°C/375°F/Gas Mark 5.
Line a baking tray with baking parchment, you'll also need an 8cm cookie cutter.

Peel and dice the pumpkin, then cook in a steamer until softened, about 10-15 minutes. Once ready, puree with a food processor, or hand blender, until you have a smooth lump-free puree, then leave to cool.

In a large bowl, cream the butter and sugar together, add the black treacle, egg and cooled pumpkin puree, and mix well together. Now sift the flour, baking powder and spice over the top, and stir in carefully to ensure all the ingredients are evenly combined and forming a dough consistency.

Wrap the dough in cling film and chill in the fridge for at least an hour.

Remove the cling film and divide the dough into 4 equally-sized portions. Roll each portion out on a floured work surface to just over ½cm thick, then use an 8cm cookie cutter to cut out your cookies, reworking the dough until it's all used up.

Place the cookies onto the prepared baking tray and bake for 6 minutes until slightly firm, but not too brown (the cooking time may need to be adjusted if you have smaller or larger sized cookies). Remove from the oven and place on a cooling rack to cool completely before tucking in, or as completely as you and anyone else within smelling distance can manage. I love these with a simple glass of cold milk. Perfect.

Pumpkin shortbread squares

EF

Makes 9 squares

250g	pumpkin
200g	soft brown sugar
1 tsp	mixed spice
130g	unsalted butter (at room temperature)
1 tsp	vanilla extract
200g	plain flour

Preheat the oven to 180°C/350°F/Gas Mark 4.
Line a 23cm x 23cm square tin with baking parchment.

Peel and dice the pumpkin, then steam until soft. When ready, after about 10-15 minutes, move the soft pumpkin to a bowl and puree with a food processor, or hand blender, until smooth. Stir in the soft brown sugar and mixed spice while the puree's still warm, then set to one side.

Now for the shortbread base
Place the butter, vanilla extract and flour into a bowl and rub with your fingertips until they form a breadcrumb texture. Now press this down evenly into the prepared tin.

Pop into the oven for 5 minutes, take out while the mixture is still soft and press it down again with the back of a spoon, so it's nicely compacted and won't crumble when it's cut. Before your shortbread goes back into the oven, it's time to add the topping.

Bringing it all together
Spread your pumpkin mixture over your shortbread base, evening it out gently with a fork or spoon. Pop back into the middle of the oven to bake for a further 15 minutes. Once cooked, place on a cooling rack and allow to cool completely before removing from the tin – it might need to be placed in the fridge if the kitchen is a bit too warm to allow it to set.

Now just cut it into squares and include in everyone's lunchbox for happy faces all round.

Pumpkin & ginger tea loaf

DF

Serves 8-10

200g	pumpkin
1	ginger tea bag
100ml	boiling water
150g	mixed dried fruit
200g	light brown sugar
3	medium free-range eggs
200g	self-raising flour
100g	ground almonds
3 tsp	ground ginger

Preheat the oven to 180°C/350°F/Gas Mark 4.
Line a 900g loaf tin with baking parchment.

Place the tea bag into a heatproof bowl, add the boiling water and leave to steep for 5 minutes, before discarding the tea bag. Now you can add the dried fruit, then set aside for 30 minutes to allow the fruit to soak in the infusion. While the fruit is soaking, peel and finely grate the pumpkin.

In a large bowl, whisk together the sugar and eggs until pale and fluffy. Gradually fold in the grated pumpkin, until nicely combined. Sift the flour, ground almonds and ground ginger onto the mix, then fold in carefully, making sure everything is thoroughly mixed. Finally, add the mixed fruit with any remaining infusion, and stir in well.

Pour the mixture evenly into the prepared tin, then pop into the middle of the preheated oven to bake for 40 minutes, until a skewer inserted into the centre of the loaf comes out clean. Place on a cooling rack for 10 minutes before taking out of the tin.

Packed with goodness

Pumpkins are such nutritious and versatile plants.

The skin, flowers, seeds and flesh are all edible

and rich in vitamins. See page144 for how to use the seeds and skin to make HEALTHY ALTERNATIVES TO CRISPS AND OTHER SNACKS.

Rhubarb & ginger ice cream

Makes 1 litre

400g	rhubarb (fresh or tinned)
20g	fresh ginger
20g	unsalted butter
2	medium free-range eggs
100g	caster sugar
100ml	milk (any kind is fine)
200ml	double cream (or your preferred non-dairy alternative)

Preheat the oven to 180°C/350°F/Gas Mark 4.
Use an ice cream maker, or make by hand in a clean 1 litre freezer-safe container.

Wash and chop the rhubarb. Peel and finely dice the ginger. Place the rhubarb and ginger into an oven-proof dish with the butter and roast in the oven until soft, about 15-20 minutes (even if using tinned rhubarb). Transfer the cooked rhubarb and ginger to a bowl, give it a good stir, then set to one side to cool.

In a separate bowl, whisk the eggs until light and fluffy. Add half the sugar and whisk again, then add the other half and whisk until everything is thoroughly combined. Now gradually add the milk, whisking as you do, then the cream, whisking gently until completely mixed in.

The cream is now ready for the cooled rhubarb and ginger to be stirred in, then place the whole lot into your ice cream maker and follow the maker's instructions.

If you're making by hand, transfer your mixture into a suitable freezer-safe container and place in the freezer for about 30 minutes, until the edges start to freeze. Take out and beat the mixture using a hand mixer or wooden spoon. By breaking up the ice cream, you're breaking up the ice crystals, which will make it smoother and creamier. Place back into the freezer and repeat after another 30 minutes, and possibly once more, until it looks and feels like ice cream.

Rhubarb & amaretti cake

Serves 8-10

300g	rhubarb
80g	unsalted butter (at room temperature)
140g	caster sugar
1	medium free-range egg
200ml	milk (any kind is fine)
275g	self-raising flour
60g	ground almonds
50g	amaretti biscuits

Preheat the oven to 180°C/350°F/Gas Mark 4.
Line a deep 18cm loose-bottomed cake tin with baking parchment.

Wash then chop the rhubarb into small chunks. Cream together butter and sugar until light and fluffy. Crack the eggs up in a separate bowl, break up with a fork, then gradually add them to the buttercream, beating until everything is nicely combined.

Now add the milk, then sift the flour and ground almonds onto the mixture, before folding in gently to ensure an even mixture. Sprinkle the chopped rhubarb over the mixture and combine with a couple of folds.

Pour the mixture evenly into your prepared tin, then pop into the middle of the preheated oven to bake for 20 minutes. While the cake is baking, crush the amaretti biscuits, ready to sprinkle over the top of the cake when it's had 20 minutes.

Once you've added the biscuit topping, pop the cake back into the oven to bake for another 20 minutes, until a skewer inserted into the centre of the cake comes out clean. Place on a cooling rack and remove from the tin after 10 minutes.

I love to eat this warmed
WITH SOME FRESH CREAM
DRIZZLED OVER THE TOP.
It's delicious.

Rhubarb Bakewell tarts

Makes 8 tarts

Sweet potato shortcrust pastry (see page 190)
Rhubarb jam (see page162)

Frangipane
100g unsalted butter (at room temperature)
100g golden caster sugar
1 tsp vanilla extract
2 large free-range eggs
120g ground almonds

To decorate
Handful of flaked almonds

Preheat the oven to 180°C/350°F/Gas Mark 4.
Lightly grease 8 x 9cm loose-bottomed flan tins. You'll also need baking beans, parchment and a 10cm round cutter.

Make the shortcrust pastry, see page190 for the recipe. Roll out the pastry until it's ½cm thick, then with the cutter, cut out 8 bases. Press the pastry bases into the prepared tins, prick each base with a fork and refrigerate for one hour.

Remove the pastry cases from the fridge, line with baking parchment and add some beans, before baking for 8 minutes. Remove the beans and baking parchment, then bake for another 5-8 minutes until golden brown, then place to one side.

While the pastry's baking, it's the perfect time to make the jam – it's deceptively simple. See page162.

Now for the frangipane
Cream together butter, sugar and vanilla extract until light and fluffy. Crack the eggs into another bowl or mug, break up and then gradually add them to the buttercream, beating as you do until everything is nicely combined. Now you can fold in the ground almonds, and you're ready to assemble.

Building your Bakewell
Spread a good layer of jam over the baked pastry cases. Spoon the frangipane cake mixture carefully and evenly over the jam, trying not to move the jam around, then sprinkle the top with flaked almonds.

Place the tins in the middle of the preheated oven to bake for 20 minutes, until golden brown and risen to a dome, then move to a cooling rack. Allow to cool before removing from the tins.

Rhubarb jam

GF OF EF SF

Makes 350g

400g	rhubarb (fresh or tinned)
2 tbsp	water
3 tbsp	chia seeds (white)
	runny honey to taste

350g sterilised jam jar or Kilner jar.
Preheat the oven to 180°C/350°F/Gas Mark 4.

If you're using fresh rhubarb, it'll need to be roasted first. Wash and cube it before placing it in a roasting tin with the water, then roast for about 20 minutes until soft. If you're using tinned rhubarb, you can miss this step out.

When the rhubarb is soft, place it in a food processor, or use a hand blender, and blitz until smooth. Add the chia seeds and blitz again for a few seconds, until everything is thoroughly combined. Have a little taste, if it's too sharp add a little honey to sweeten, blitzing again for a few seconds to combine.

When you're happy your jam is sweet enough, pour it into the sterilised jar, and that's it. It couldn't be simpler. The jam will keep for up to a week in the fridge.

If possible, use white chia seeds. Black taste just fine, but you tend to see the seeds.

Did you know...?
While many people consider rhubarb a fruit
IT'S ACTUALLY A VEGETABLE.
And the redder the stalk
the sweeter the taste.

Rhubarb & raspberry meringue cake

Rhubarb meringue cake is a classic German dessert, known as the easy to get your tongue around Rhabarberkuchen. I've adapted this favourite and added a little raspberry twist.

Serves 8-10

400g	rhubarb
150g	unsalted butter (at room temperature)
150g	caster sugar
3	medium free-range eggs
100ml	milk (any kind is fine)
280g	self-raising flour
60g	raspberries

Meringue

3	medium free-range egg whites (at room temperature)
100g	caster sugar

Preheat the oven to 160°C/325°F/Gas Mark 3.
Line a 20cm round springform cake tin with baking parchment.

Wash and chop the rhubarb, fresh works best for this recipe, into small chunks. Cream the butter and sugar together until light and fluffy.

Crack the eggs into a separate bowl, break up with a fork, then gradually add them to the buttercream, beating until thoroughly mixed. Next gradually beat in the milk. Then sift the flour on top, before gently folding in until everything is nicely combined.

Pour evenly into your prepared tin and sprinkle with the chopped rhubarb and raspberries. Leave to one side while you make the meringue.

Now to get cracking with the meringue
In a clean bowl whisk the egg whites briskly, or on high if you're using a mixer, until they form soft peaks. Gradually add the sugar, a tablespoon at a time, whisking as you do.

Spoon the meringue on top of your prepared fruit-topped cake mix. Pop the compiled cake into the middle of the preheated oven and bake for 40-50 minutes, until the meringue is golden brown. You can check the cake is cooked by gently slipping the skewer at an angle into the cake to see if it comes out clean.

When the cake is cooked, place on a cooling rack to cool completely before carefully lifting out of the tin.

Tips for a successful meringue

Make sure your bowl and whisk are completely clean, dry and grease free.

Use eggs at room temperature, they're easier to whisk.

SEPARATE YOUR EGGS CAREFULLY TO AVOID ANY YOLK GETTING IN – IT CONTAINS FAT WHICH WILL REDUCE THE NICE VOLUME YOU'RE AFTER.

Once the egg whites have formed soft peaks, add the sugar gradually to ensure a lovely smooth consistency.

DON'T WAIT TO BAKE.
THE MERINGUE WILL DEFLATE OVER TIME.

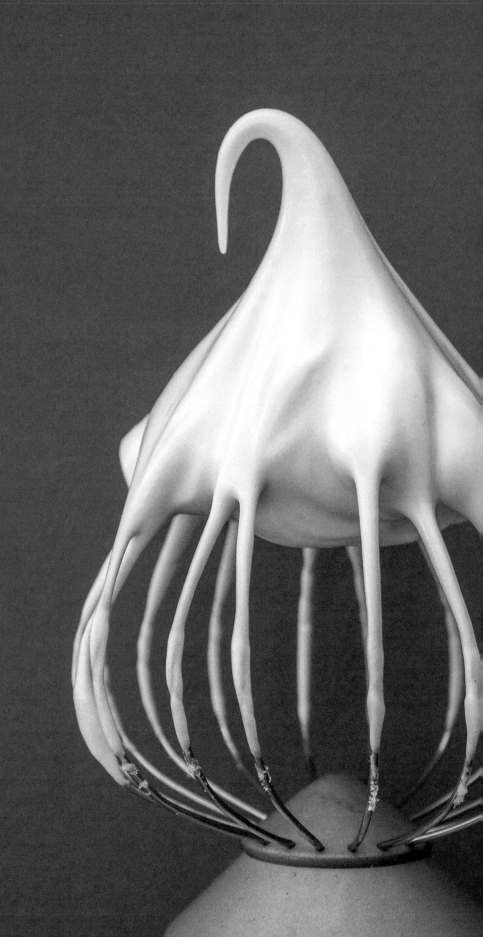

Spinach & blackcurrant meringue pie

Two nutrient-dense powerhouses come together in one lip-smacking pie.

Serves 8-10

Sweet potato shortcrust pastry (see page 190)

Blackcurrant filling

400g	blackcurrants
250g	spinach
3 tbsp	chia seeds
	runny honey to taste

Meringue

4	large free-range egg whites (at room temperature)
170g	caster sugar

Preheat the oven to 180°C/350°F/Gas Mark 4.
Grease a 20cm loose-bottomed tart tin. You'll also need baking beans and parchment.

Make up the shortcrust pastry, see page 190. Roll out the pastry to ½cm thick and line your tart tin. Prick the bottom with a fork, lay a sheet of round greaseproof paper on the base and fill with baking beans, then pop into the fridge to chill for 20 minutes.

While the pastry's taking things easy, add the blackcurrants, spinach and chia seeds to a food processor, or use a hand blender, and blitz until smooth, adding honey to taste if desired.

Pop the pastry into the oven to bake for 10 minutes, then remove the beans and paper and bake again for a further 5 minutes until light brown. Set to one side on a cooling rack.

In a clean dry bowl, whisk the egg whites until they form soft peaks, then continue whisking as you slowly add the sugar, 1 tablespoon at the time, until the meringue is glossy and forms soft peaks.

Spoon the blackcurrant and spinach mixture into the cooked pastry case. Now very gently spread the meringue over the top, covering all of the filling. Place the pie in the preheated oven and bake for 30-40 minutes, until the meringue is light brown and crispy. Move to a cooling rack once cooked.

Double whammy goodness

I love the **CONTRAST OF THE RICH BERRIES WITH THE LIGHT MERINGUE,** *and get asked to make this a lot. The fruity berries work so well with the* **protein-rich spinach,** *and together pack a double whammy of iron.*

SNAP UP THE GOODNESS

SPINACH IS BEST USED AS SOON AS POSSIBLE
– *it loses nutritional goodness with every passing day.*
While keeping it in the fridge will slow this,
half of the major nutrients will still be lost within
eight days of it being picked.

Spinach & pistachio ice cream

Makes 1 litre

150g	spinach
150g	pistachios
100ml	milk (any kind is fine)
100g	caster sugar
2	medium free-range eggs
200ml	double cream (or your preferred non-dairy alternative)

Use an ice cream maker, or make by hand in a clean 1 litre freezer-safe container.

Wash and then steam the spinach for 5 minutes, until soft. Transfer to a food processor or hand blender and blitz until you have a nice smooth puree. Set to one side to cool.

Finely grind 100g of the pistachios in a food processor, or crush in a mortar and pestle. Place in a saucepan with 50ml of milk and 50g of sugar, and gently bring to the boil, stirring to dissolve the sugar. Remove from the heat as soon as it comes to the boil. Stir in the spinach puree and leave to cool.

In a separate bowl, whisk the eggs until light and fluffy. Add half of the remaining sugar and whisk again, then add the other half and whisk until all is thoroughly combined. Now you can gradually add the remaining milk, then the cream, whisking gently as you do until everything is thoroughly mixed.

Now just stir in your cooled spinach and pistachio puree, then place the whole mixture into your ice cream maker and follow the maker's instructions.

If you're making by hand, transfer your mixture into a suitable freezer-safe container and place in the freezer for about 30 minutes, until the edges start to freeze. Take out and beat the mixture using a hand mixer or wooden spoon. By breaking up the ice cream, you're breaking up the ice crystals, which will make it smoother and creamier. Place back into the freezer and repeat after another 30 minutes, and possibly once more, until it looks and feels like ice cream.

Finish with the last 50g of pistachios, crushed and sprinkled on top.

Spinach loaf

Serves 8-10

250g	spinach
180ml	olive oil
2 tbsp	lemon juice
1½ tsp	vanilla extract
3	medium free-range eggs
200g	caster sugar
220g	plain flour
3 tsp	baking powder

Preheat the oven to 180°C/350°F/Gas Mark 4.
Line a 900g loaf tin with baking parchment.

Wash and steam the spinach until soft, then transfer to a mixing bowl and puree until it's silky smooth. Add the olive oil, lemon juice and vanilla extract, and mix well. Crack the eggs into the mixture and beat in well, before adding the sugar and mixing again.

Sift the flour and baking powder onto the mixture, then gently fold in until everything is thoroughly combined.

Pour the mixture into the prepared loaf tin and pop into the middle of the preheated oven to bake for 20 minutes, or until a skewer inserted into the centre of the loaf comes out clean. Move to a cooling rack and leave for 10 minutes before removing the tin.

This is based on a Turkish recipe, and would traditionally be finished with lemon icing, but it's up to you. Personally, I think it's delicious as it is, or with a lovely strong Turkish coffee.

Super spinach

One of nature's most PROTEIN-RICH
VEGETABLES, *spinach is also packed with
essential vitamins & minerals, including*

vitamins C, B2, B6, E, K *&* A

*(in the form of carotenoids), manganese, folate,
magnesium, iron, copper, calcium and potassium.*

TALK ABOUT PACKING A

DO-YOU-GOOD PUNCH!

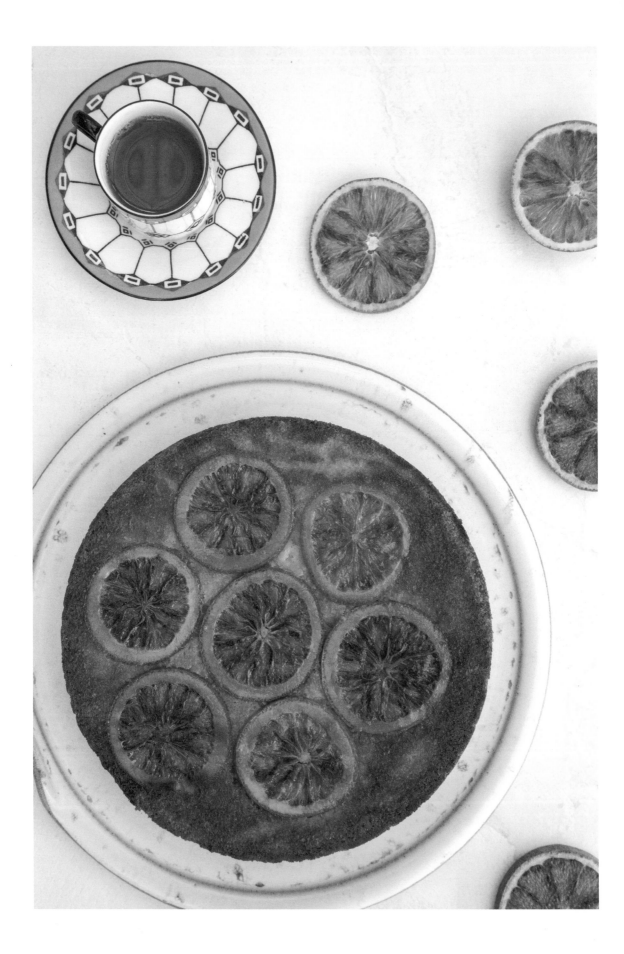

Swede & blood orange cake

Serves 8-10

200g	swede
180g	unsalted butter (at room temperature)
180g	caster sugar
3	medium free-range eggs
50g	plain yogurt
50g	self-raising flour
180g	ground almonds
1 tsp	baking powder

Oranges

50ml	water
100g	caster sugar
2	blood oranges, sliced thinly using a mandolin or sharp knife

Preheat the oven to 160°C/320°F/Gas Mark 3.
Line a 20cm round springform cake tin with baking parchment.

Peel and finely grate the swede. Place the water and sugar into a saucepan and stir over a low to medium heat until the sugar has dissolved. Now turn the heat up to medium high, add the blood orange slices and bring to the boil. Once boiling, simmer for 10-15 minutes, until the peel becomes semi-translucent. Using a slotted spoon, transfer the orange slices to a plate to cool.

Boil the remainder of the syrup until thick, stirring occasionally to make sure it doesn't burn. Once ready, allow the syrup to cool a little. Then, using a pastry brush, paint a fine coating of the syrup over your prepared tin and arrange the orange slices – this will become the top of your cake. You can set the rest of the syrup to one side for now.

In a large bowl, cream the butter and sugar until light and fluffy. Crack the eggs into a separate bowl or mug, break up with a fork, then gradually add them to the buttercream, beating as you do. Now stir in the yogurt, fold in the grated swede, then sift the flour, ground almonds and baking powder on top and gently fold into the mixture.

Spoon the mixture evenly into your prepared tin, taking care not to move the orange slices. Pop into the middle of the preheated oven and bake for 40-45 minutes, until a skewer inserted into the centre of the cake comes out clean. Move to a cooling rack for at least 15-20 minutes before turning out onto a plate. Brush the top and sides of the cake with the remaining syrup, and that's it, your masterpiece is complete.

Spiced swede cake

Serves 8-10

150g	swede
150g	runny honey
3	medium free-range eggs
50g	unsalted butter (at room temperature)
1 tsp	vanilla extract
150g	gram flour
1 tsp	baking powder
1½ tsp	mixed spice

Preheat the oven to 180°C/350°F/Gas Mark 4.
Line a 23cm round cake tin with baking parchment.

This spiced delight is super easy to make. Start by peeling, dicing and then steaming the swede until soft, then puree with a food processor, or hand blender, until smooth.

In a large bowl, whisk the honey, eggs, butter and vanilla extract together until it has a smooth, light and fluffy consistency. Add the pureed swede and fold in. Now sift the gram flour, baking powder and mixed spice on top, then gently fold in.

Pour into the lined tin and pop into the middle of the preheated oven to bake for 40 minutes, until a skewer inserted into the centre of the cake comes out clean. Keep an eye on your cake while it's baking, you might need to place a piece of baking parchment on top to stop it from browning too much.

When it's ready, place on a cooling rack for 10 minutes before taking out of the tin, then leave to cool completely, or for as long as you can keep tempted fingers away. The aroma is incredible.

Swede & orange ice cream

Makes 1 litre

200g	swede
2	large unwaxed oranges – juice & zest
2	medium free-range eggs
100g	caster sugar
100ml	milk (any kind is fine)
200ml	double cream (or your preferred non-dairy alternative)

Use an ice cream maker, or make by hand in a clean 1 litre freezer-safe container.

Peel and cube the swede, then steam for 15 minutes or until soft. Transfer to a food processor or hand blender, add the orange juice, then blitz until you have a nice smooth puree. Set to one side to cool.

In a large bowl, whisk the eggs until light and fluffy. Add half the sugar and whisk again, then add the other half and whisk until everything is thoroughly combined. Gradually add the milk, whisking as you do, then the cream, again while whisking, until all the ingredients are completely combined.

Fold in the pureed swede and orange zest, then place the whole lot into your ice cream maker and follow the maker's instructions.

If you're making by hand, transfer your mixture into a suitable freezer-safe container and place in the freezer for about 30 minutes, until the edges start to freeze. Take out and beat the mixture using a hand mixer or wooden spoon. By breaking up the ice cream, you're breaking up the ice crystals, which will make it smoother and creamier. Place back into the freezer and repeat after another 30 minutes, and possibly once more, until it looks and feels like ice cream.

Imagine an orange

Swede was used as a substitute for orange juice in World War II.
It must have taken some imagination though!

FOR A CHANGE, TRY A MIX OF...
100g swede and 100g carrot, this also goes really well
with the orange juice in this recipe.

Sweet potato & apricot flapjacks

EF

Whenever we have a picnic, I always get asked to bring these.

Makes 12 slices

200g	sweet potato
200g	unsalted butter
50g	caster sugar
2 tbsp	runny honey
100g	chopped apricots
250g	rolled oats

Preheat the oven to 180°C/350°F/Gas Mark 4.
Line a 20cm x 20cm square tin with baking parchment.

Peel and finely grate the sweet potato. Place the butter, sugar and honey into a saucepan over a low heat to melt gently. Once melted, stir in the grated sweet potato, mixing well. Add the chopped apricots and mix well, then half the oats, mixing well, then the second half of the oats and give it all another good stir.

Tip the mixture into the lined tin and press down really well with a back of a spoon – if you don't press down well, your flapjacks will be too crumbly to pick up. Place on the middle shelf of the preheated oven to bake for 20 minutes, until golden brown. Move to a cooling rack and leave to cool completely before removing from the tin, then just cut into squares or slices.

These are ideal to make in advance, and store well in an airtight container for up to 7 days.

Sweet potato & blackberry ice cream

Makes 1 litre

400g	purple sweet potato
300g	blackberries
2	medium free-range eggs
100g	caster sugar
100ml	milk (any kind is fine)
200ml	double cream (or your preferred non-dairy alternative)

Preheat the oven to 180°C/350°F/Gas Mark 4.
Use an ice cream maker, or make by hand in a clean 1 litre freezer-safe container.

Wash, towel dry then prick the skins of the sweet potatoes, then pop into the preheated oven to bake for 30 minutes, until soft in the centre. When cool enough to handle, scoop out the flesh, discarding the skins, then blitz with the blackberries, using a food processor or hand blender, until you have a smooth paste. Finish by pushing the paste through a sieve to ensure you have a super smooth sauce, then set to one side to cool.

In a separate bowl, whisk the eggs until light and fluffy. Add half the sugar and whisk again, then add the other half and whisk until evenly combined. Gradually add the milk, then the cream, whisking gently as you do. Now just stir in your sweet potato and blackberry puree, and it's ready to turn into ice cream.

Place the mixture into your ice cream maker and follow the maker's instructions.

If you're making by hand, transfer your mixture into a suitable freezer-safe container and place in the freezer for about 30 minutes, until the edges start to freeze. Take out and beat the mixture using a hand mixer or wooden spoon. By breaking up the ice cream, you're breaking up the ice crystals, which will make it smoother and creamier. Place back into the freezer and repeat after another 30 minutes, and possibly once more, until it looks and feels like ice cream.

Sweet potato blondie cake

Makes 12 squares

200g	sweet potato (white sweet potato is best for this)
200g	white chocolate
75g	unsalted butter
2	medium free-range eggs
100g	caster sugar
1 tsp	vanilla extract
180g	self-raising flour

Preheat the oven to 180°C/350°F/Gas Mark 4.
Line a 20cm x 20cm square tin.

Peel and dice the sweet potato, steam until soft, then puree with a food processor or hand blender until you have a smooth lump-free texture. Leave to one side to cool.

Place 100g of the chocolate and all of the butter into a bain-marie to slowly melt together. If you don't have a bain-marie, use a heatproof bowl over a steaming saucepan of water, making sure the bowl doesn't touch the water. Once the chocolate and butter have melted, remove from the heat, add to the sweet potato puree, mix well, then set aside to cool.

In a separate bowl, whisk the eggs, sugar and vanilla extract together, then add to the cooled chocolate mixture. Sift the flour on top and fold in, ensuring everything is nicely combined. Now chop the remaining chocolate into chunks and stir into the mixture.

Pour evenly into the prepared tin and pop into the middle of the preheated oven to bake for 20-30 minutes, until the centre is firm. Place on a cooling rack until completely cooled before removing from the tin. Dust with icing sugar and cut into squares.

PICK THE RIGHT POTATO

WHITE SWEET POTATOES *aren't as sweet as orange and purple sweet potatoes,* **making them ideal for this recipe.**

Sweet potato chocolate chip cookies

Makes 12 cookies

150g	sweet potato
125g	unsalted butter (at room temperature)
100g	caster sugar
1	large free-range egg – yolk only
1 tsp	vanilla extract
225g	plain flour
40g	white chocolate chips
40g	milk chocolate chips

Preheat the oven to 180°C/350°F/Gas Mark 4.
Line a baking tray with baking parchment. You'll also need an 8cm cookie cutter.

Peel and dice the sweet potato, steam until soft, then puree until it's smooth and lump free.
Set aside to cool.

In a separate bowl, cream the butter and sugar together until light and fluffy. In another bowl
or a mug, break up the egg yolk with a fork. Gradually beat the egg into the buttercream. Now
stir in the cooled sweet potato puree and vanilla extract.

Sift the flour on top, then fold in, again making sure everything is nicely mixed. Add the
chocolate chips and give it one last mix. Now all that's left to do is to work it into a ball
using your hands.

Transfer the dough to a lightly floured surface and roll out to ½-1cm thick. Cut out your
cookies with a cookie cutter, or cut them out roughly by hand, which I think gives them a
lovely uneven handmade look. Rework your dough each time it's too full of holes, and keep
going until you have a small ball left, which you can squash to make the last cookie.

Place your cookies onto the lined baking tray and bake in the middle of the preheated
oven for 15 minutes, until a lovely golden colour. Place on a cooling rack and allow to cool
completely before eating – only kidding, I've never yet seen these get cold before at least one
was 'tested'.

My daughter Hannah thinks every cake or cookie is
MADE WITH VEGETABLES. *When making cookies
one day, she proudly announced that she was going to put
sweet potato into her cookies today.* **They were so good,**
I wanted to share her recipe with you.

Sweet potato pancakes

Makes 12 pancakes

200g	sweet potato
568ml	dairy-free milk (or cow's milk if you prefer)
2	medium free-range eggs
1 tsp	vanilla extract
20g	runny honey
160g	buckwheat flour
½ tsp	mixed spice
	oil (any kind is fine)

Medium sized, about 18cm, frying pan.

Peel and dice the sweet potato, then steam until soft. Puree with a food processor or hand blender until lovely and smooth, then set aside to cool.

Add the milk, eggs, vanilla extract and honey to the cooled sweet potato puree and mix until thoroughly combined. Sift the flour and mixed spice on top, then mix again ensuring any lumps are gone.

To cook your pancakes

Now you have your batter, it's time to get pancake making. Wipe a medium-sized frying pan or crêpe pan with an oiled kitchen towel. Place on a medium heat, then when the pan's hot, add enough pancake batter to cover the base.

Cook your pancakes for 1 minute on each side until golden. If you're feeling brave, you can flip your pancake to cook the other side. If you're not, use a big spatula or fish slice to turn your pancake over.

Delicious served with lemon wedges, maple syrup, marrow and apple butter (page 98) or jam (see pages 24 and 162 for my recipes).

Sweet potato shortcrust pastry

Everyone comments on how wonderful my pastry is. So much so, that this is now my go-to shortcrust pastry recipe. People are still in total amazement when I say it's made with sweet potato.

Makes enough for a 23cm tin

120g sweet potato
100g unsalted butter (at room temperature)
250g plain flour
20g caster sugar

Peel and steam the sweet potato, then puree with a food processor or hand blender until nice and smooth (it's a good idea to do this the day before and keep it in the fridge – it's easier to use chilled, and gives better results).

In a food processor, add the sweet potato puree, butter, flour and sugar, then pulse until it looks like breadcrumbs. You can do this by hand, rubbing the ingredients together with your fingertips, but it can take a while and your hands need to be cold.

Tip the crumb mixture onto your work surface, then use palms of your hands to press the mix until it forms a firm ball of dough, handling the pastry as little as possible. Now just wrap it in cling film and place in the fridge for an hour.

You now have delicious ready-to-go shortcrust pastry, perfect for a tasty tart with a twist.

Try SWAPPING SWEET POTATO
for another vegetable,

such as beetroot or spinach,

FOR RED OR GREEN PASTRY.

Sweet potato & chocolate fudge slice

Makes 12-15 slices

200g	sweet potato
40g	unsalted butter
100g	caster sugar
1	large free-range egg
2 tsp	vanilla extract
60g	self-raising flour
40g	cocoa powder
6 tbsp	milk (any kind is fine)

Chocolate fudge frosting

55g	unsalted butter
1 tbsp	milk (any kind is fine)
2 tbsp	cocoa powder
75g	icing sugar

Preheat the oven to 180°C/350°F/Gas Mark 4.
Line a 20cm x 20cm square tin with baking parchment.

Peel and dice the sweet potato, then steam until soft. Transfer to a food processor, or a bowl with a hand blender, and puree until smooth and lump free. Set aside to cool.

Melt the butter in a saucepan over a low heat, then remove from the heat and stir in the sugar and pureed sweet potato, mixing well.

In a separate bowl, whisk the egg and vanilla extract, then set to one side. When everything has cooled, add the whisked egg to the pureed sweet potato and mix well. Sift the flour and cocoa powder on top, then fold in, before gradually adding the milk and folding in, making sure everything is evenly mixed.

Pour into the prepared tin and pop into the middle of the preheated oven to bake for 10-15 minutes, until a skewer inserted into the centre of the cake comes out clean. Once cooked, place on a cooling rack and leave in the tin to cool.

A tempting topping

As if this wasn't tempting enough, we're going to top it off with a delicious Chocolate fudge frosting. Add the butter and milk to a saucepan and melt over a low heat, stirring occasionally.

Sift the cocoa powder and icing sugar into a bowl, make a well in the middle, then pour in the melted butter and milk. Stir thoroughly to combine. Now just pour over the cooled cake to finish your fudge slice, and leave to set before cutting into slices.

It's easy to get helpers when making this cake, who wouldn't want to lick the spoon when you're finished?

TO EXTEND THE LIFE OF YOUR VEGETABLES

LINE THE BOTTOM OF YOUR FRIDGE VEGETABLE DRAWERS **with paper towels.** The towels will absorb the excess moisture that causes vegetables to go bad.

Sweetcorn & blueberry clafoutis

A clafoutis is a rustic French dessert traditionally made by baking black cherries in a custard-like mix, similar to a pancake batter. This inspired my clafoutis with a sweetcorn and blueberry twist.

Serves 8-10

250g	sweetcorn (fresh, tinned or frozen)
2 tbsp	milk (any kind is fine)
100g	unsalted butter
100g	runny honey
2	medium free-range eggs
200g	self-raising flour
1 tsp	baking powder
100g	blueberries

Preheat the oven to 180°C/350°F/Gas Mark 4.
Line a 24cm oblong tin with baking parchment.

Steam the sweetcorn until soft, then transfer to a food processor, or a bowl with a hand blender, add the milk and puree until smooth.

Place the butter and honey into a saucepan over a low heat, and melt gently until the butter is liquid. Transfer to a mixing bowl and leave to cool. Once cooled, add the eggs and mix well, then stir in the sweetcorn and milk blend. Now sift the flour and baking powder directly onto the mixture, beating well to ensure everything is completely combined.

Pour the mixture evenly into the prepared tin, scatter with blueberries and pop into the middle of the preheated oven to bake for 25-30 minutes, until a skewer inserted into the centre comes out clean. Move to a cooling rack and leave to cool completely before lifting from the tin.

This super-soft tasty treat really needs to be eaten the day it's baked, it goes a bit flat if left any longer.

Sweetcorn & honeycomb ice cream

Makes 1 litre

Ice cream

2	corn on the cob (frozen or tinned are fine too)
100ml	milk (any kind is fine)
2	medium free-range eggs
100g	caster sugar
200ml	double cream (or your preferred non-dairy alternative)

Honeycomb

4 tbsp	golden syrup
1 tbsp	water
200g	caster sugar
1½ tsp	bicarbonate of soda

Use an ice cream maker, or make by hand in a clean 1 litre freezer-safe container. You'll also need a 20cm x 20cm tin, thoroughly greased.

Strip the corn off the cob. To do this, hold an ear of corn on its end, and with a sharp knife, cut downwards with a sawing motion. Don't worry about getting right up against the cob. Continue in strips around the cob until all of the corn has been removed.

Place the corn in a saucepan with the milk, bring to the boil then simmer for 10 minutes. Leave in the milk to cool, which further allows the corn to infuse the milk. Then pour the corn and milk into a food processor or blender, and blitz until you have a smooth paste. Finish by pushing it through a sieve to ensure your puree is lovely and lump free.

In a separate bowl, whisk the eggs until light and fluffy. Add half the sugar and whisk again, then add the other half and whisk until thoroughly combined. Now slowly add the cream and whisk gently until mixed in. Finally, stir in your sweetcorn puree, and you're ready to place the mixture into your ice cream maker and follow the maker's instructions.

If you're making by hand, transfer your mixture into a suitable freezer-safe container and place in the freezer for about 30 minutes, until the edges start to freeze. Take out and beat the mixture using a hand mixer or wooden spoon. By breaking up the ice cream, you're breaking up the ice crystals, which will make it smoother and creamier. Place back into the freezer and repeat after another 30 minutes, and possibly once more, until it looks and feels like ice cream.

Making your honeycomb

Place the golden syrup, water and sugar into a saucepan, bring to the boil then simmer for about 8 minutes, making sure it doesn't burn. Remove from the heat and drip a little bit into cold water. You'll know the mixture is ready when it becomes brittle in the water. Now add the bicarbonate of soda, stirring quickly as it will foam up. Then pour the mixture into your tin and set to one side to cool and go hard.

When the ice cream is ready, break up the honeycomb and mix into the ice cream.

Sweetcorn lemon curd

Makes 350g

200g	sweetcorn (fresh, frozen or tinned are all fine)
1	unwaxed lemon – zest
50ml	lemon juice
2	medium free-range egg yolks
	maple syrup to taste

350g sterilised jam jar or Kilner jar.

Steam the sweetcorn until soft, then puree in a food processor or hand blender until it's as smooth as you can get it. Remove any husks by pushing the sweetcorn through a sieve.

Add the lemon zest, juice and egg yolks, mix well, then warm in a saucepan over a low heat until the mixture thickens. Add maple syrup to taste.

Pour the curd into the sterilised jar. It'll keep for up to a week in the fridge, and makes a really pretty, very delicious gift.

This makes the perfect accompaniment

TO A WARM BATCH OF

PARSNIP & HONEY SCONES.

I love using this ice cream to

MAKE A FREAK SHAKE

decorated with fresh raspberries,

my daughters and their friends love it.

Tomato & raspberry ice cream

Makes 1 litre

200g	red tomatoes
200g	fresh raspberries
2	medium free-range eggs
100g	caster sugar
100ml	milk (any kind is fine)
200ml	double cream (or your preferred non-dairy alternative)

Use an ice cream maker, or make by hand in a clean 1 litre freezer-safe container.

Score the tomato skins and pour some boiling water over them, then leave them to rest in the water for 10 minutes until the skin starts to peel. Carefully remove from the hot water and gently peel the skin off.

Place the tomatoes and raspberries into a food processor or blender, and blitz to a smooth paste. To make sure you've got all the pips out, push the paste through a sieve for a super smooth sauce.

In a large bowl, whisk the eggs together until light and fluffy. Add half the sugar and whisk again, add the other half and whisk once more, until everything is nice and smooth and well combined. Gradually add the milk, whisking gently as you do, then the cream, still whisking gently until everything is completely mixed in.

Now just stir in your tomato and raspberry puree, and when it's all combined, transfer to your ice cream maker and follow the maker's instructions.

If you're making by hand, transfer your mixture into a suitable freezer-safe container and place in the freezer for about 30 minutes, until the edges start to freeze. Take out and beat the mixture using a hand mixer or wooden spoon. By breaking up the ice cream, you're breaking up the ice crystals, which will make it smoother and creamier. Place back into the freezer and repeat after another 30 minutes, and possibly once more, until it looks and feels like ice cream.

Tomato & strawberry tarte Tatin

EF

When I first told my family I was going to combine tomatoes and strawberries in a tarte Tatin, the silent reply was deafening. I baked it anyway and left it on the side. It quietly disappeared, with just one question, when was I going to bake another one? It's delicious!

Serves 6-8

200g	sweet cherry tomatoes
200g	strawberries
100g	unsalted butter
75g	caster sugar
275g	puff pastry (ready-made is just fine)

Preheat the oven to 200°C/400°F/Gas Mark 6.
Use a 23cm ovenproof frying pan.

Cut the tomatoes and strawberries in half. Melt the butter in the frying pan, then add the sugar and stir until dissolved. Now add the tomatoes and strawberries, neatly and tightly arranged around the pan in an attractive design, they'll become the top and decoration of your tarte Tatin.

Cook the tomatoes and strawberries over a low heat for 15 minutes, until they begin to caramelise, resisting the temptation to stir or disturb them.

To distract yourself, roll out the puff pastry on a lightly floured surface until it's nice and round and slightly larger than the frying pan. When the tomatoes and strawberries are ready, gently place the puff pastry circle on top and tuck in the edges.

Place the frying pan in the middle of the preheated oven and bake for 15-25 minutes, until the pastry has risen and turned a lovely golden colour. Move the frying pan to a cooling rack and leave to cool for 5 minutes, before running a knife gently around the edge of the pastry.

When it's ready, place a plate on top of the frying pan, carefully turn it all over, and abracadabra, you have a fabulously colourful tarte Tatin. Serve warm or cold with ice cream, it's truly scrumptious.

A FRUITY LITTLE NUMBER
TOMATOES ARE IN A FACT A FRUIT.
*So it's much less of a surprise that cherry tomato
and strawberry make such a fabulous combination.*

WELL I NEVER KNEW THAT...
The Tatin, in a tarte Tatin, *is actually the surname
of the sisters said to have created this delicious dish.*

Yellow tomato loaf

Serves 8-10

250g	yellow tomatoes
130g	unsalted butter (at room temperature)
100g	caster sugar
2	large free-range eggs
200g	self-raising flour
1 tsp	baking powder
1 tsp	mixed spice

Preheat the oven to 180°C/350°F/Gas Mark 4.
Line a 900g loaf tin with baking parchment.

Skin and deseed the tomatoes. To do this, simply score the skin with a cross, then place the tomatoes into a bowl of freshly boiled water and leave until the skin starts to peel back. Carefully lift out the tomatoes and gently peel the skin back, it should come off quite easily. Then halve and deseed the tomatoes, leaving just the lovely yellow flesh.

Place the tomatoes into a bowl and puree until smooth. In another bowl, cream the butter and sugar until light and fluffy.

Crack the eggs into a bowl and break up with a fork, then add to the buttercream beating the mixture as you do to ensure a lovely even texture. Add the tomato puree and gently fold in. Now sift the flour, baking powder and mixed spice over the top, and gently fold in until all the ingredients are nicely combined.

Pour into the lined loaf tin and pop onto the middle shelf of the preheated oven to bake for 40 minutes, until a skewer inserted into the centre of the cake comes out clean. Place on a cooling rack for 10 minutes before lifting out of the tin to finish cooling.

I love to have this with a cup of jasmine tea, it perfectly complements the very delicate flavour of the cake.

TOO MUCH OF A GOOD THING? NEVER!

A glut of these lovely orange tomatoes led me to get my thinking hat on.
My family were feeling a bit over-tomatoed, until I created this cake, then
THEY WERE MORE THAN HAPPY TO KEEP EATING THEM.

Turnip & coconut Bundt

Turnip is such an underrated and underused vegetable, which I think is a shame. This cake won't fail to impress and is so easy to make, I hope it encourages more people to give the turnip a try.

Serves 8-10

200g	turnip
150g	unsalted butter (at room temperature)
160g	caster sugar
4	medium free-range eggs
3 tbsp	desiccated coconut
200g	self-raising flour

Icing

100g	icing sugar
20ml	coconut cream

Preheat the oven to 180°C/350°F/Gas Mark 4.
Thoroughly grease a 20cm Bundt tin.

Peel and finely grate the turnips. In a separate bowl, cream the butter and sugar until light and fluffy. Now crack the eggs into another bowl, and break up with a fork, then gradually add to the mix, beating as you do. Next add the grated turnip and desiccated coconut and fold in, ensuring everything is well mixed. Now sift the flour on top, and fold in until everything is nicely combined.

Pour the mixture evenly into the prepared Bundt tin and pop into the middle of the preheated oven to bake for 40 minutes, until a skewer inserted into the centre of the cake comes out clean. Once cooked, move to a cooling rack and leave to cool completely before turning out.

The finishing touch

When your cake has cooled, you can start on the decoration, which will transform the Bundt into a swirl of light, fluffy coconut slices. Start by adding the coconut cream to the icing sugar and beating until smooth, then carefully pour the icing between the cake folds.

Simple, yet incredibly effective and wonderfully tasty. I don't think the humble turnip has ever looked or tasted so good.

Turnip & pineapple upside-down cake

Serves 6

180g	turnip
150g	self-raising flour
100g	unsalted butter (at room temperature)
100g	caster sugar
2	large free-range eggs
6	pineapple rings (tinned or fresh are fine)
6	glacé cherries

Preheat the oven to 180°C/350°F/Gas Mark 4.
Grease a 6 hole jumbo muffin pan.

These fun muffins couldn't be much easier to make, and once the turnip has been prepared, is an ideal recipe to make with children.

Peel, dice and steam the turnip until soft. Blitz in a food processor or with a hand blender until smooth, then set aside to cool.

In a separate bowl, beat together the flour, butter, sugar and eggs until nice and smooth.

Place a pineapple ring into each of the muffins holes, with a cherry in the middle, then pour the mixture evenly into the muffin holes.

Bake on the middle shelf of the preheated oven for 20 minutes, until a skewer inserted into the centre of a muffin comes out clean. Leave on a cooling rack, only lifting out of the tin when completely cooled.

GREEN EYED MONSTER

This recipe works well with other colourful vegetables. Try spinach or kale for

green upside-down cakes

that make fantastic

Halloween monster eyes.

Turnip yule log

Serves 8-10

Roll

100g	turnip
70g	caster sugar
3	medium free-range eggs
60g	self-raising flour
2 tbsp	cocoa powder

Filling

80g	unsalted butter (at room temperature)
175g	icing sugar
1 tsp	vanilla extract

Icing

Avocado & chocolate icing (see page 14)

Preheat the oven to 200°C/400°F/Gas Mark 6.
Line a 33cm x 23cm Swiss roll tin with baking parchment.

Peel, dice and steam the turnip until soft, then blitz in a food processor or with a hand blender until smooth. Leave to one side to cool.

Whisk the sugar and eggs together until light and fluffy. When it's cool, fold in the turnip puree. Sift the flour and cocoa powder on top, then gently fold in until nicely combined.

Pour the whole lot evenly into the prepared Swiss roll tin. Pop into the middle of the preheated oven to bake for 8-10 minutes, until a skewer inserted into the centre comes out clean.

When it's ready, carefully turn the cake out onto a lightly sugared piece of greaseproof paper. Peel off the baking parchment and neaten the edges with a quick trim, if required. Allow the sponge to cool for 3 minutes – don't let it go cold or it'll be difficult to roll.

Score one short side with a sharp knife, about 1cm in from the edge, then using the greaseproof paper, roll up from the scored side. Rest it, with the seam on the bottom, to finish cooling.

Now for the filling
Cream the butter, icing sugar and vanilla extract in a bowl until light and fluffy.

The final stage, building your yule log
Unroll the sponge then, using a palette knife, spread the filling evenly over the inner surface. Using the greaseproof paper, carefully roll the sponge back up, placing it seam-side down again. Cut the end diagonally and place it on the side of the roll, to make it look like a V-shaped log.

Cover with avocado and chocolate icing, then use a fork to score lines to make it look like bark. Finish with a snow-like dusting of icing sugar.

I'll bet you're feeling festive now.

Zucchini & cinnamon sponge

Serves 6-8

220g	zucchini (courgette)
150g	caster sugar
140ml	sunflower oil
2	large free-range eggs
240g	self-raising flour
½ tsp	baking powder
1 tsp	ground cinnamon
30g	walnuts (chopped)

Preheat the oven to 180°C/350°F/Gas Mark 4.
Line a deep 20cm round loose-bottomed tin.

This cake looks, smells and tastes great, and is super easy to make. Start by washing and finely grating the courgettes.

In a separate bowl, whisk the sugar, oil and eggs until they're light and fluffy. Add the grated courgette and fold in until they're nicely combined. Sift the flour, baking powder and cinnamon on top and gently fold in, again making sure everything is well mixed.

Pour the mixture into the prepared tin and scatter the walnuts on top, before popping into the middle of the preheated oven to bake for 40 minutes, until a skewer inserted into the centre of the cake comes out clean.

When the cake is ready, remove from the oven and place on a cooling rack for 10 minutes before taking out of the tin. And that's it. No need for decoration or fanfare. Perhaps just a wee pat on the back and a generous slice with a big mug of tea or coffee.

I had great fun choosing a name for this book.
*In the end, the idea for **Cakes with Secret Ingredients from A to Z** was the perfect fit. There was only one problem, in England we don't have a vegetable starting with Z. But they do in America, Australia, Italy, Germany and other parts of the world, so in came zucchini, and suddenly we have cakes with secret ingredients and an international flavour.*

Zucchini & orange pancakes

Makes 8 pancakes

180g	courgette, or zucchini if you prefer
2	unwaxed oranges – juice & zest
2	large free-range eggs
60g	caster sugar
570ml	milk (any kind is fine)
240g	self-raising flour
2 tsp	baking powder
	oil (any kind is fine)

Small, about 14cm, frying pan.

Wash and finely grate the courgettes, mind your fingers on the grater! Zest and juice the oranges.

Mix the eggs, sugar and milk together in a mixing bowl. Stir in the grated courgette, orange juice and zest, making sure they're well mixed. Sift the flour and baking powder onto the mixture and stir in, making sure everything is thoroughly combined.

Warm a small frying pan, wipe with a kitchen towel dampened with a little oil of your choice. Now just pour in a couple of tablespoons of the mixture and cook for about 1½ minutes. Turn over and cook on the other side for 1 minute – flipping the pancake between sides if you're feeling adventurous, or turning with a fish slice or spatula if you're not.

Then slide onto a plate, ideally warmed, and serve with the topping of your choice. I like these on their own – they're delicious, while my husband loves them with orange segments and plain yogurt.

Zucchini & chocolate loaf

DF

Serves 8-10

250g	courgette, or zucchini as it's also known
180g	dark chocolate (70% minimum cocoa solids)
170ml	sunflower oil
100g	caster sugar
2	large free-range eggs
200g	self-raising flour
1 tsp	baking powder

Choice of two toppings:

Avocado & chocolate icing (see page 14)

or

Dark chocolate topping

100ml	double cream (or your preferred non-dairy alternative, to keep it dairy free)
150g	dark chocolate (70% minimum cocoa solids)

Preheat the oven to 180°C/350°F/Gas Mark 4.
Line a 900g loaf tin with baking parchment.

While the oven's preheating, quickly break up the dark chocolate into a heatproof bowl, with the sunflower oil, and pop it into the oven to warm through.

Wash and finely grate the courgette. Then, when the chocolate's melted, carefully take the bowl out of the oven and stir in the grated courgette. Leave to cool.

In a separate bowl, whisk the sugar and eggs until light and fluffy. When the courgette and chocolate mixture has cooled a little, fold it into the sugar and eggs, ensuring everything is evenly mixed. Sift the flour and baking powder on top and gently fold in, again making sure everything is thoroughly combined.

Pour the mixture evenly into the prepared tin and pop into the middle of the preheated oven to bake for 50 minutes, until a skewer inserted into the centre of the loaf comes out clean. Leave on a cooling rack for 15 minutes before taking out of the tin.

For a flourish to finish

Pour the cream into a saucepan and bring to the boil. While it's coming to the boil, break the chocolate into chunks and place in a heatproof bowl. When the cream's ready, pour it over the chocolate, stirring until the chocolate's melted and the mix is completely smooth.

Leave to cool and thicken, then place your cake onto a serving plate and pour the chocolate liberally over the top. Simple yet very effective. Now just try to make sure you get the biggest slice – well it is the cook's privilege after all!

Candied vegetables

As a rough guide, I allow 100g of vegetables to nicely decorate an average sized cake, but you may like more or less decoration, so it really is up to you. You can use virtually any vegetables.

Just some of the vegetables that are great candied
carrot
parsnip
butternut squash
pumpkin
beetroot
fennel

For each 100g of vegetables you will also need
100g   caster sugar
100ml water

Preheat the oven to 140°C/280°F/Gas Mark 1.
Line a baking sheet with baking parchment.

Carefully cut the vegetables into fine ribbons, a mandolin is ideal for this task, or failing that a sharp knife. Just take care with both.

Warm the sugar and water in a saucepan, over a medium heat. When the sugar has dissolved, turn up the heat and bring to the boil. Add the vegetable ribbons, maintaining a rolling boil.

After 3 minutes, lift the vegetables out with a slotted spoon (be careful as they'll be very hot). Lay the ribbons on the lined baking sheet, then pop into the preheated oven to bake for 20 minutes.

When they're ready, take out of the oven. While the ribbons are still hot, they can be twisted into patterns and shapes. You'll have to work fast though, as they harden quickly, but you can always pop them back into the oven for a couple of minutes to soften again if needed.

Allow to dry thoroughly before placing in an airtight container. These will store for 14 days, plenty of time to get baking.

Stopping your colours running

It's best to boil the lightest colours first, in batches, building up to the darkest, especially if you're using beetroot, or everything will turn red.

Jam tarts

Makes 12 tarts

batch   sweet potato shortcrust pastry (see page 190)
batch   jam (see pages 24 and 162 for recipes)
           flour for dusting

Preheat the oven to 180°C/350°F/Gas Mark 4.
Lightly grease a 12 hole tart tin.
You'll also need a round cutter to match the size of your tart tin.

Make the shortcrust pastry, using the recipe on page 190. Also make the jam of your choice, see pages 24 or 162.

Dust your work surface with a little flour, unwrap and roll out the chilled pastry, so that it's no more than ½cm thick.

Use the round cutter to cut out 12 pastry circles, making sure the circles are big enough to line the holes of the tin. Spoon 1-2 teaspoons of jam into each of the pastry cases.

Place in the middle of the preheated oven to bake for 15-18 minutes, until the pastry is golden brown and the filling is starting to bubble a little. Leave to cool in the tin for a few minutes before carefully transferring to a wire rack to cool completely.

These quintessentially British tea time *treats make a lovely introduction to baking for little people, if you* MAKE THE PASTRY AND JAM FOR THEM FIRST. *You can even cut out pastry decorations for the tops,* things like love hearts, stars, moons and initials.

Mince pies

Makes 24 pies

batch   sweet potato shortcrust pastry (see page 190)
batch   mincemeat (see page 52)
2 tbsp milk
          flour to dust the board

Preheat the oven to 180°C/350°F/Gas Mark 4.
Lightly grease a 12 hole tart tin.
You'll also need a round cutter to match the size of your tart tin, 8cm is
fairly typical.

Make the shortcrust pastry in readiness, and chill in the fridge until needed – see page 190
for the recipe. For my carrot mincemeat recipe, see page 52.

Dust your work surface with a little flour, unwrap and roll out the chilled pastry so it's no more
than ½cm thick. Using the round cutter, cut out 12 circles big enough to line the holes of the
tin, then cut out 12 lids, you might want to use a smaller cutter for this.

Place 1-2 teaspoons of mincemeat into each of pastry case. Place the lids on top and press
down lightly around the edge. Brush the top with some milk, then make a couple of small
holes in each lid for any steam to escape.

Pop into the middle of the preheated oven to bake for 15-18 minutes, until golden brown.
Place on a cooling rack for a few minutes, while still in the tin, then carefully transfer your
pies to a wire rack to finish cooling.

If you're feeling in the mood, why not try some different types of pastry top, perhaps a lattice,
strips, decorative pastry holly leaves, stars, unicorns… let your imagination run riot!

I CAN NEVER MAKE ENOUGH
of **these mince pies,** *they're*
so popular *with* **FAMILY & FRIENDS.**

Rainbow cake

Serves 10-12

180ml	olive oil
2 tbsp	lemon juice
3	medium free-range eggs
200g	caster sugar
220g	plain flour
3 tsp	baking powder

*Please note, these are the ingredients for **one** layer, you'll need to multiply by 6 for the whole cake.*

Colours

for the six vegetable food colours see page 230

Icing

450g	icing sugar
500g	cream cheese

Preheat the oven to 180°C/350°F/Gas Mark 4.
Line a 23cm springform cake tin with baking parchment for each coloured layer.

In a large mixing bowl, add the olive oil and lemon juice, then mix well until nicely combined. Now crack the eggs into a separate bowl or jug, break them up with a fork, then stir into the mix. Next comes the sugar, with another good stir to ensure everything is nicely combined.

Now you can stir in the first of your six vegetable colours (see page 230) mixing it well so that it's evenly distributed throughout the cake mixture. Finally, sift the flour and baking powder on top, then fold in gently, ensuring everything is thoroughly and evenly combined.

Pour the mixture into your prepared tin and bake in the centre of the preheated oven for 30-40 minutes, or until a skewer inserted into the centre of the cake comes out clean. Once cooked, move to a cooling rack for 10 minutes before lifting out of the tin, leave to cool. So that's one colour done, now just repeat for each of the remaining five colours.

To decorate

For your icing, simply cream the icing sugar and cream cheese together in a bowl. The icing needs to be fairly firm for the cake to hold, so you may need to add some more icing sugar.

Assembling your rainbow

Neaten the tops of the sponges where needed, then spread icing over the top of each cake and stack, starting with violet, blue, green, yellow, orange and finally red on the top, saving some icing to decorate the outside. Now just spread the remaining icing gently over the top and sides, and hey presto, one amazing vegetable rainbow cake.

I'm not saying this is easy, but the cake shown here was
MADE ENTIRELY *by my 14-year-old daughter,* GEMMA.
She had a lot of fun making it too.

Natural food colourings

GF OF EF V RS/SF

Red

250g	beetroot
	– raw or vacuum packed
	– peeled & cubed
50g	raspberries
2 tsp	white wine vinegar

If the beetroot is raw, steam it until soft. Place in a bowl with the raspberries and white wine vinegar, puree until smooth, then for a super smooth finish, push through a sieve to remove any raspberry pips.

Orange

250g	carrot
	– peeled & chopped

Steam the carrot until soft, then transfer to a mixing bowl and puree until silky smooth.

Yellow

250g	sweet potato
	(orange variety)
	– peeled & cubed

Steam the sweet potato until soft, then move to a bowl and puree until silky smooth.

Green
250g   spinach

Blue
250g   red cabbage
        – finely sliced
50ml   water
1 tsp   bicarbonate of soda

Violet
250g   sweet potato
        (purple variety)
        – peeled & cubed

Wash then steam the spinach until wilted, this only takes a few minutes, then place in a mixing bowl and puree until silky smooth.

Steam the red cabbage until soft, then move to a mixing bowl and puree until silky smooth. Finally, add the bicarbonate of soda and watch the magic happen.

Steam the sweet potato until it's nice and soft, then just transfer it to a mixing bowl and puree until silky smooth.

Seasonal vegetables

I think few things taste better than seasonal ingredients that have ripened naturally in the sun or soil. They're often cheaper, fresher, and if you're buying locally-grown, support your local growers too.

SPRING
Mar–May

asparagus, cauliflower, cucumber,
purple sprouting broccoli, radish,
rhubarb, spinach, spring greens

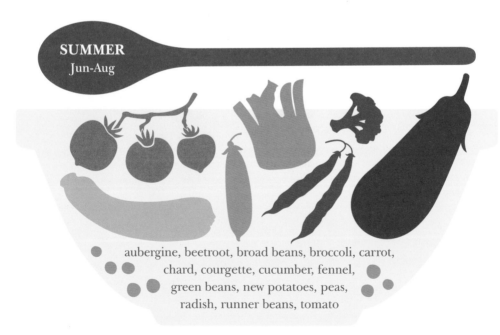

SUMMER
Jun–Aug

aubergine, beetroot, broad beans, broccoli, carrot,
chard, courgette, cucumber, fennel,
green beans, new potatoes, peas,
radish, runner beans, tomato

AUTUMN
Sept-Nov

beetroot, butternut squash, carrot,
celeriac, kale, leek, marrow, potato, pumpkin,
sweetcorn, sweet potato, tomato

WINTER
Dec-Feb

beetroot, brussels sprouts, cauliflower, chicory,
Jerusalem artichoke, parsnip, red cabbage,
savoy cabbage, swede, turnip

Kate's top tips

Always read the recipe in full before beginning.

This is a simple tip, but such an important one. Reading ahead will help you to know the how, why, where and when of what you are about to make. It only takes a couple of minutes to read a recipe, but could potentially mean the difference between a great bake and a sorry failure.

TO AVOID A CAKE RACK IMPRINT ON YOUR CAKE, **place a tea towel over the rack** *before turning the cake out onto it.*

If you're using orange, lime or lemon zest, **USE UNWAXED FRUITS.** *The lovely gloss comes from wax sprayed onto the fruit to keep it looking fresh, and to help protect it during transportation. If you can't find unwaxed fruit, just scrub the skin first,* **the wax comes off** *quite* **easily.**

Sterilising your jam jars

When making jam you need to ensure your jars are scrupulously clean and sterilised. **Heat the oven to 140°C/275°F/Gas Mark 1.** Wash your jars with hot soapy water, rinse well, then place on an ovenproof tray in the oven for 20 minutes. Leave to cool first before you fill them. *If you're using Kilner jars, remove and boil the rubber seals separately, as dry heat damages them.*

Using ingredients AT ROOM TEMPERATURE gives better results.

For instance, **cold eggs won't** WHIP UP *as easily – they don't hold the same volume of air as warm eggs,*

& you'll get more juice from warm citrus fruit.

COOKING SPINACH INCREASES ITS HEALTH BENEFITS! **One cup** *of cooked spinach will give you* **three times the nutrients of a cup of raw spinach.** *This is because the body can't completely break down and use the nutrients in raw spinach.*

Roast beetroot before adding it to your cakes **– it brings out the beet's natural caramel flavour.** *Roasted beetroot goes particularly well with* **dark chocolate's depth** *of flavour.*

Are you cutting your cake correctly?

*British mathematician, Francis Galton, explains how it should be done to keep your cake fresher longer, in his letter **"Cutting a Round Cake on Scientific Principles"** published in 1906. It goes like this:*

1. Central segment is removed and the two remaining halves pushed back together.

2. Central segment is removed, at a 90° angle to the first segment.

3. The four remaining segments are pushed back together ready to cut the next central slice.

Run out of self-raising flour?

Just add one teaspoon of baking powder to every 125g of plain flour, but make sure you sift thoroughly to combine.

MAKE CARROT CAKE
WITH A TWIST

– swap the carrot for grated sweet potato, pumpkin or parsnip for a change.

Has your milk gone a bit 'over', is it slightly soured or curdled? If it's not thick or lumpy, DON'T THROW IT AWAY, *it's perfect to use as buttermilk in scones or pancakes.*

A quick way to check if your eggs are still fresh enough to use is to pop the egg into a bowl of water – if it sinks it's fresh and good to use, if it floats or bobs to the surface, it's bad – don't eat it!

**bobbing = bad
sinking = safe**

Baking powder – don't add too much!

If the recipe states 1 teaspoon, carefully add 1 teaspoon, levelling the spoon first.
IF YOU ADD TOO MUCH, THE CAKE COULD RISE,
FALL QUICKLY & THEN DRY OUT.
Baking powder can also leave a faint metallic taste to the cake if you use too much.

Index A-Z *of cakes with secret ingredients*

Key

 Gluten Free

 Dairy Free

 Egg Free

 Vegan

 **Refined Sugar Free**

Recipes containing raw egg are unsuitable for pregnant women, elderly, very young or those with impaired immune systems.